Curriculum Theory

Third Edition

CURRICULUM THEORY

Third Edition

GEORGE A. BEAUCHAMP
Northwestern University

THE KAGG PRESS   Wilmette, Illinois   1975

Library of Congress Catalog Card Number: 74-25800
ISBN Number: 0-912200-05-7
Printed in the United States of America

To Kathryn

PREFACE

The first serious effort to bring together ideas about curriculum theory was a conference held at the University of Chicago in 1947. Approximately ten years later, it occurred to me that it would be fruitful to examine carefully the status of curriculum theory with particular reference to its dimensions and processes. The examination culminated in the first edition of *Curriculum Theory* in 1961. Thereafter, a growing number of persons became interested in curriculum theory, and they produced a larger volume of literature than had been written before on the subject. Those circumstances motivated me to write the second edition of *Curriculum Theory* in 1968. Since 1968, professional interest in curriculum theory has been sustained, and the number of interested scholars has continued to grow. This continuous growth of interest has compelled the preparation of this third edition.

Similar procedures were followed in the research effort for this book as were followed in preparing earlier editions. A fresh look was taken at literature describing practices and concepts relating to theory development in behavioral disciplines related to education for cues leading to a discussion of curriculum theory. Next, cues were sought from efforts in theory development within the broad field of education in the belief that curriculum theory must be a subtheory of educational theory. A third step consisted of noting milestones in the development of ideas about curriculum theory. The results are presented in Chapters 1 through 4. Finally, an analysis was made of the theoretical issues, problems, and alternatives within identified components of curriculum theory. These areas are discussed in Chapters 5 through 8. Chapter 9 contains an outline of my curriculum theory as it has evolved to the present time.

I must thank several persons for assistance with this

publication. In former editions, Wilbur Yauch, Gail Inlow, and Joe Park gave substantial assistance in the development of manuscripts. Much of their effort is reflected in this book. For this edition in particular, I shall forever be indebted to my colleagues Patricia Conran and Gregory Mullen for their patience and their yeoman efforts in reading and criticizing the manuscript as it was developed. Susan Chrystal, Laurel Ittelson and Maud Hall patiently helped with typing and proofreading. I sincerely thank those authors and publishers who consented to the use herein of materials either paraphrased or directly quoted. Proper credits are given in the text.

My wife, Kathryn, has been an invaluable partner in this entire effort. Only the smallest portion of my gratitude is expressed through dedicating the book to her.

George A. Beauchamp
Evanston, Illinois

TABLE OF CONTENTS

Curriculum Theory

Third Edition

Chapter 1

CURRICULUM THEORY AS AN EDUCATIONAL PROBLEM

A book on curriculum theory should stimulate theory-building activity that goes beyond conjecture and speculation. For too long, education in the United States has developed as a technology rather than as a science. This is to say that most of what we do in schools has come about more from our experience in the practical affairs of running schools than from well-developed theories which would give greater and more systematic meaning to the practices. This is not to say that practical experience can be ignored. In fact, Gordon and others explain the value of practice or tradition for stimulating more scientific guides to behavior:

> Often, in the early days of the development of a scientific area, folklore typically provides a better basis for guiding behavior than scientific theory. However, history shows that once substantial effort has been devoted to the development of an area of knowledge, scientific means of prediction and control rapidly surpass those which tradition has provided.[1]

One reason for this reliance on tradition might be that schools in our country have been very close to the people. This characteristic is a natural result of demand for mass education with the attendant problems of teacher supply and school construction. Each time in our history that a crisis has confronted the public schools, the technology has become more complicated. Whenever a demand

---

[1] Ira J. Gordon (ed.). *Criteria for Theories of Instruction* (Washington, D.C.: Association for Supervision and Curriculum Development, N.E.A., 1968), p. 6.

for the transmission of an element of our culture to the young has arisen, that element often has become a new school subject. And most of the time, these subjects have been added without clear definition of pupil needs or the changing role of the school that demands new subjects. Examples like drug and sex education, consumer education, and environmental education are a few that have become popular subjects in the curriculum of the public schools. These have grown by the additive process, with social pressures being in large part responsible. Ours is a trial-by-error approach to educational or curricular innovation rather than a rational approach grounded in theory.

Contrast this procedure with areas of human effort where practices and well-developed theories have a reinforcing relationship. Our scientists and social scientists have developed theories to direct practices and to explain relationships. The theories are modified by technology and research, but they also tend to direct much of the technological development.

In education there has been too little employment of the techniques of science in the development of theories. One reason may be that such an approach appears to many to be impersonal and devoid of values. The products of the scientist tend to be impersonal, but as Conant pointed out, the activities of the scientists are shot through with value judgments.[2] An alternative way to state this argument is to use the philosophy of science expression *theory-determined* or *theory-laden*. Some might wish to say that all phenomena are perceived from a particular perspective and what the scientist sees is necessarily limited by theories he holds to be representative of reality; that is, "what a man sees depends upon what he looks at and also upon what his previous visual-conceptual experience has taught him to see."[3]

Another deterrent to the use of scientific techniques is inherent in the scientific process. Kuhn illustrates the time-lag problem:

> . . . discovering a new sort of phenomenon is necessarily a complex event, one which involves recognizing both *that* something is and *what* it is . . . . if both observation and conceptualization, fact and assimila-

---

[2]James B. Conant, *Modern Science and Modern Man* (Garden City, N.Y.: Doubleday and Company, Inc., 1952), p. 107.

[3]Thomas S. Kuhn, *The Structure of Scientific Revolutions* (2d ed., enl.; Chicago: The University of Chicago Press, 1970), p. 113.

tion to theory, are inseparably linked in discovery, then discovery is a process and must take time.[4]

Educators have been concerned with empirical data of all kinds, but they have been unable to make use of the conceptual processes of science in the development of theories. Some explanation may be found in the rapid growth of education in a growing country in which schools have been faced with one crisis after another. The contradiction between the practices of crisis hopping at a survival level and the time consuming *that* and *what* discovery processes of theorizing is self-evident. Another explanation may be found in the lack of ability and interest of educators in theory-building work. Explicit rationales for the operations of schools are urgently needed lest chaos be created by diversity in practice. Herein lies another difficulty for educators who are always searching for a model, or paradigm, that works in their particular situation. But paradigms are rarely replicable from one field to another in their original form. Skills and procedures need to be developed for their application and adaptation. In any case, the day seems to be past when the development of theory in education can continue to ignore the procedures of science.

CURRICULUM THEORY IN PERSPECTIVE

However, the central theme of this book is not educational theory but curriculum theory. Any educational theory would have to account for all the known components of education including curriculum. We probably should distinguish between education and schooling because most curriculum practice is a function of schooling. That is, a curriculum is developed for a school, and the processes of planning it and implementing it take place in the environment of the school. On the other hand, theory development in curriculum functions at a broader level than curriculum practices. It has to do with knowledge production in professional education. Hence, curriculum theory is a sub-theory of educational theory.

All theory is interdisciplinary in the sense that theories are developed by using many common rules and processes and by borrowing and adapting paradigms among fields. To the extent

---

[4]*Ibid.*, p. 55.

that theory building has been more vigorous and experienced over a longer period of time in the basic disciplines, all theories derive from the established disciplines. Figure 1 depicts a cluster of theory relationships; in essence, it is a theory microcosm of which curriculum theory is a part. At the top of the figure, three basic content categories of theory appear; they consist of the humanities, the social sciences, and the natural sciences. Within these three categories, the various established disciplines, such as English, sociology, or physics, have developed theories designed to explain and predict relationships within their respective provinces of knowledge. Scholars in the disciplines were first in developing theories. They borrowed paradigms and procedures from one another, and in turn, those who would develop theories in areas not classified as disciplines likewise borrowed and adapted from the basic disciplines. This is why we can say that all theory is interdisciplinary.

Emerging from these broad categories of theory are theories in the applied areas of knowledge. These are shown at the second level of the figure, with architecture, engineering, education, law, and medicine used as examples. Theories in the applied areas of knowledge draw their primary authority and information from the basic disciplines. However, it is true that a field such as engineering will draw primarily from the natural sciences, law from the social sciences, and so forth. Even though theories in applied areas derive greatly from the theories of the disciplines, they may not be considered to be sub-theories to the discipline theories; they do not support, or they are not an integral part of the disciplines.

Beginning with the applied areas, however, each group of theories is undergirded by a series of sub-theories. In other words, theories in architecture, engineering, education, law, or medicine normally would be supported by a structure of sub-theories. The chart does not include sub-theories for architecture, engineering, law, or medicine. The illustrative sub-theories for education are administrative theories, counseling theories, curriculum theories, instructional theories, and evaluation theories. These will be discussed in later chapters, but for now it is sufficient to make the point that substantive theories tend to be supported by clusters of sub-theories.

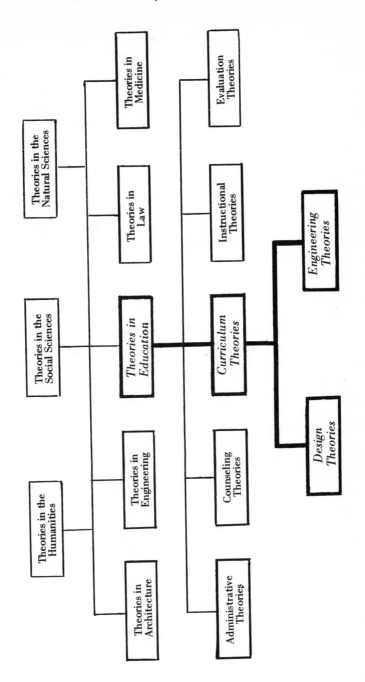

Figure 1. *Curriculum theory in perspective.*

Our focus of attention in this book is upon curriculum theories; therefore, in the diagram, solid lines have been used to identify and to show direct connections between supra- and sub-theories of curriculum. Most attention, therefore, must be spent upon theories in education, curriculum theories, design theories, and engineering theories. Although theories in law or engineering may contribute to administrative theories or curriculum theories, they are of secondary importance to this discussion since all of the groups of theories listed at the third level are sub-theories to theories in education. Similarly, at the fourth level in the chart, administrative theories, counseling theories, instructional theories, and evaluation theories are of secondary importance to this discussion. They may influence curriculum theories, and they may influence the sub-theories of curriculum. Again, the chart does not include sub-theories for administrative, counseling, instructional, or evaluation theories because our main line of concern has to do with the theory domains boxed in by heavy lines. What Figure 1 does is show vividly how curriculum theory is an educational problem. Curriculum theory is a necessary link in a series of events which in combination explain education.

CONCEPTS IN CURRICULUM THEORY

The specific dimensions of curriculum theory reside in the concepts and derived generalizations that are unique to the field of curriculum. At least in the very early stages of his work, a theorist must concentrate upon the identification of the most important concepts in his field. In this way, he delimits the subject matter of his field of work. When relationships among concepts are established as generalizations, the scientific theorizer begins to form a classification scheme for phenomena within his field. This state of affairs is what Braithwaite referred to as a natural history stage in the development of science.[5] Perhaps this is the stage in which curriculum theory is at the present moment because those who exhibit interest in curriculum are striving to define their basic concepts and to establish relationships among them.

Chief among the problems for the curriculum theorist, however, is the establishment of precise meanings associated with

[5]Richard B. Braithwaite, *Scientific Explanation* (New York: Harper and Row, 1960), p. 1.

the basic concepts of curriculum. The words have been chosen, but the meanings to be attributed to them are diffused. The important term for curriculum theory is *curriculum*. From a theoretical point of view, it is impossible to develop subordinate constructs, or relationships, with other components of education, until ground rules are laid down through meanings ascribed to the basic term *curriculum*.

In my opinion, there are three ways in which the term curriculum is most legitimately used. An individual, for instance, may legitimately speak of *a curriculum*. A curriculum is a written document which may contain many ingredients, but basically it is a plan for the education of pupils during their enrollment in a given school. It is the overall plan that is intended to be used by teachers as a point of departure for developing teaching strategies to be used with specific classroom groups of pupils. A second legitimate use of the term curriculum is to refer to *a curriculum system* as a sub-system of schooling. A curriculum system in schools is the system within which decisions are made about what the curriculum will be and how it will be implemented. A third legitimate use of the term curriculum is to identify *a field of study*. Persons most concerned with curriculum as a field of study are undergraduate and graduate students enrolled in professional education work at colleges and universities, professors of curriculum, and curriculum theorists.

There are other interpretations associated with curriculum, but they are difficult to relate to the three so briefly described here. For example, curriculum and instruction frequently are depicted as interchangeable terms. At other times, instruction is conceived to be part of curriculum, or curriculum is thought to be subordinate to instruction. When terms are intermingled in this way, communication is complicated, and it is difficult for anyone to develop research designs that can penetrate the profuse number of variables involved.

With so many uses and interpretations of curriculum as the basic concept in the field, it is easy to imagine the confusion that reigns among subordinate concepts. The problem for organized thinkers in the area is to search out the relationships that need to be established and which will lead to explanatory and predictive generalizations. In the process, operational constructs can be developed that will clarify many of the subordinate concepts within curriculum.

All of these matters constitute the specific dimensions of curriculum theory as an educational problem, and thus they are the subject matter of this entire book. The plan of presentation in this book essentially follows Figure 1. The next chapter contains an examination of basic principles of theoretical work derived from those disciplines related to education. Chapter 3 is a discussion of theory developments in education. Chapters 4 through 8 contain detailed discussions of the more specific dimensions and problems of theory building in curriculum beginning with developments in curriculum theory, followed in order by discussions of values as determinants in curriculum decisions, curriculum design, curriculum engineering, and curriculum as a field of study. In the final chapter, I have tried to set forth the principal ingredients of my curriculum theory as it has evolved up to now. Admittedly, it is incomplete in many details, but it does set forth the rudiments of one explanation for that series of events we call curriculum.

It is hoped that this treatment of curriculum theory will stimulate two kinds of activity — more precise theory building and more theoretically-oriented research. Theory-building efforts will help to identify gaps in our knowledge. Theoretically-oriented research will help to fill in those gaps. In this way, we can move away from a purely technological operation and toward a behavioral science. Certainly, if there is any hope for developing a discipline of education, sub-theories of education such as curriculum theories will have to be built using the skills and the procedures of the social scientist. It is also hoped that any ideas or procedures herein presented will be checked, challenged, and/or repeated by others who are concerned with the growth of curriculum theory.

Chapter 2

THEORY BUILDING

The purpose of this chapter is to identify the basic issues and procedures in theory building as background for considerations of similar work in the field of curriculum. In the following pages, we will review the meanings that have been associated with the word "theory" and identify some of the primary functions, structures, and processes associated with theory building by those who have labored at theory construction. We may use as paradigms the experiences of those who pioneered in the natural and social sciences, particularly the social sciences. We and they are bound by certain common rules of behavior in theorizing, and the primary reason for search into what others have done is to learn what those rules are. The common rules of theorizing then will be applied to past and future developments briefly in educational theory and then more thoroughly in curriculum theory since curriculum theory is our principal concern in this book.

Whenever scholars have lacked experience in theory development in a field of endeavor, it has been customary for them to look to the patterns set by those who have been successful and to use those patterns as paradigms for beginning efforts. Since there have been but meager efforts at theory construction and use in education, those who would do theory building in education need to find ways of borrowing, relating, and associating the theoretical experiences of other social scientists as beginning focal points for their own efforts. As an applied social science, education must look to original sources in the established social science disciplines for guiding structures, processes, and rules. Parsons gave support to this kind of borrowing in theory development in human affairs when he indicated: ". . . good general theory in the field of human action, no matter how firmly grounded in one discipline, is inevitably interdisciplinary theory."[1]

THEORY DEFINED

There is general agreement that a theory is a set of related statements explaining some series of events, but as one might expect, there are disagreements about what the character of the statements should be. As stated by Logan and Olmstead:

> Everyone agrees that a theory is, among other things, a set of statements; there is disagreement about what other characteristics any set of statements must have in order to be labeled "theory."[2]

Statements about sets of events differ greatly in complexity. In part, the variation is due to the scope of the series of events. In part, it is due to the degree of sophistication with which the set of events has been treated by theorists in the field of endeavor. In spite of these differences, nearly all serious writers on theory have defined the term one way or another. Some example definitions of theory will help to illustrate convergent and divergent viewpoints about the meanings associated with theory. It appears that theory definitions may be characterized by one or more of three dimensions: unifying statements, universal propositions, and/or predictive statements.

Most definitions of theory express unification of phenomena within the set of events encompassed by the theory. Kaplan expressed it thus:

> A theory is a way of making sense of a disturbing situation so as to allow us most effectively to bring to bear our repertoire of habits, and even more important, to modify habits or discard them altogether, replacing new ones as the situation demands. In the reconstructed logic, accordingly, theory will appear as the device for interpreting, criticizing, and unifying established laws, modifying them to fit data unanticipated in their formation, and guiding the enterprise of discovering new and more powerful generalizations.[3]

---

[1]Talcott Parsons, "General Theory in Sociology," *Sociology Today,* edited by Robert K. Merton, Leonard Broom, and Leonard S. Cottrell, Jr. (New York: Basic Books, Inc., 1959), p. 37.

[2]Frank Logan and David Olmstead, *Behavior Theory and Social Science* (New Haven: Yale University Press, 1955), p. 4.

[3]Abraham Kaplan, *The Conduct of Inquiry* (San Francisco: Chandler Publishing Company, 1964), p. 295.

Brodbeck compared theoretical and common language when she wrote:

> Language consists of words and sentences. To the *words* of ordinary speech correspond the *concepts* of science; to the *sentences* its *definitions*, its *statements* of *individual fact* and *of laws*. Certain sets of sentences constitute the *theories* of science.[4]

Hall and Lindzey stated that a theory is a set of conventions that "should contain a cluster of relevant assumptions systematically related to each other and a set of empirical definitions."[5] O'Connor noted that in contrasting theory from practice we ". . . refer to a set or system of rules or a collection of precepts which guide or control actions of various kinds."[6] Snow summarized his concept of a theory when he stated:

> In its simplest form, a theory is a symbolic construction designed to bring generalizable facts (or laws) into systematic connection. It consists of a) a set of units (facts, concepts, variables) and b) a system of relationships among the units.[7]

Rudner defined theory as ". . . a systematically related set of statements, including some lawlike generalizations, that is empirically testable."[8] From such definitions one catches the spirit of theory as a unifying phenomenon. The idea of "set" as a homogeneous group of statements seems to be a basic concept in theorizing.

The character of a set of statements making up a theory is delimited when the definition of a theory specifies what kinds of statements are demanded and how they are to be derived. A definition by Rose illustrates:

> A theory may be defined as an integrated body of definitions, assumptions, and general propositions covering a given subject matter from which a comprehensive and consistent set of specific and testable hypotheses can be deduced logically.[9]

---

[4]May Brodbeck, "Logic and Scientific Method in Research on Teaching," *Handbook of Research on Teaching*, N.L. Gage, editor (Chicago: Rand McNally and Company, 1963), pp. 44-45.

[5]Calvin S. Hall and Gardner Lindzey, *Theories of Personality* (2d ed.; New York: John Wiley and Sons, Inc., 1970), p. 11.

[6]D.J. O'Conner, *An Introduction to the Philosophy of Education* (London: Routledge and Kegan Paul, 1957), p. 75.

[7]Richard E. Snow, "Theory Construction for Research on Teaching," *Second Handbook of Research on Teaching*, Robert M. W. Travers, editor (Chicago: Rand McNally & Company, 1973), p. 78.

[8]Richard S. Rudner, *Philosophy of Social Science* (Englewood Cliffs, N.J.: Prentice-Hall, Inc., 1966), p. 10.

[9]Arnold M. Rose, "Generalizations in the Social Sciences," *American Journal of Sociology*, 59:52, August, 1953.

By these criteria, the set of statements would include definitions, assumptions, and general propositions with specified relational properties. On a somewhat more complicated level, theories are related to laws, hypotheses, and logico-mathematical deductions. Abel used the following words to voice his interpretation of general theory in the social sciences:

> A general theory is built upon the facts discovered by means of the use of theorems and other conceptual models from empirical data and which have been expressed in the form of laws, correlations, or other types of generalizations. It involves synthesis and is directed to the formulation of propositions about universals.[10]

Feigl's frequently quoted definition is in a similar vein, but it is more detailed.

> I propose to define a "theory" as a set of assumptions from which can be derived by purely logico-mathematical procedures, a larger set of empirical laws. The theory thereby furnishes an explanation of these empirical laws and unifies the originally relatively heterogeneous areas of subject matter characterized by those empirical laws. Even though it must be admitted that there is no sharp line of demarcation (except a purely arbitrary one) between theoretical assumptions and empirical laws, the distinction, at least in the sense of gradation, is illuminating from a methodological point of view.[11]

In addition to the two dimensions of unification and universal propositions, a third needs to be added to complete the characterization of theory definitions, and that is the dimension of prediction. Some theorists choose to define theory so that prediction is the key dimension. For example, Travers noted that a theory consists of generalizations intended to explain phenomena and that the generalizations must be predictive.[12] Actually, a full definition of theory satisfies all of these characteristics. Kerlinger combined all of the dimensions that have been mentioned when he wrote the following:

> A theory is a set of interrelated constructs (concepts), definitions, and propositions that present a systematic view of phenomena by specify-

---

[10]Theodore Abel, "The Present Status of Social Theory," *American Sociological Review*, 17:162, April, 1952.

[11]Herbert Feigl, "Principles and Problems of Theory Construction in Psychology," *Current Trends in Psychological Theory* (Pittsburgh: University of Pittsburgh Press, 1951), p. 182.

[12]Robert M. W. Travers, *An Introduction to Educational Research* (3rd ed.; New York: The Macmillan Company, 1969), p. 10.

ing relations among variables, with the purpose of explaining and predicting the phenomena.[13]

These various definitions of theory lead to the tentative conclusion that there must be different kinds of theories derived by different processes. We will explore this notion in the following sections on the structures, functions, and processes in theory building.

STRUCTURAL ELEMENTS OF THEORY

We can further expand our insights and understandings of theory building by examining briefly the principal structures and functions of theories. Figure 2 is a representation of a generalized set of events that normally constitutes a theory. In Figure 2, the

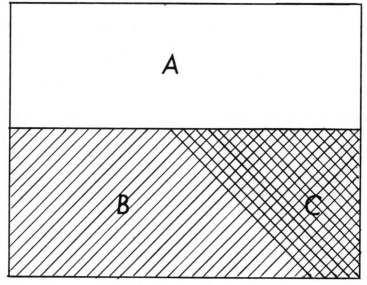

ABC = *The universal set*
A = *Events of known dimensions*
B = *Events of assumed dimensions*
C = *Events of unknown dimensions*

Figure 2. *A set of events constituting a theory.*

---

[13]Fred N. Kerlinger, *Foundations of Behavioral Research* (2d ed.; New York: Holt, Rinehart and Winston, Inc., 1973), p. 9.

universal set represented by ABC is the set of events to be
explained by the theory. The universal set is subdivided into three
subsets: A, B, and C. Subset A represents those events of known
dimensions, which might be expressed as statements of fact, law, or
principle. Subset B represents those events of assumed
dimensions, which might be expressed as assumptions,
propositions, postulates, or in some other way to reflect tentative
information that does not reach the pinnacle of certainty
exemplified by fact or law. Subset C represents those events that
are part of the universal, or total, set of events for which adequate
explanation is not yet available. The task of the theorist is to
formulate terms and statements that will explain the contents of
the various subsets of the theory and to show their
interrelationships.

Terms

A crucial aspect of a scientist's work is his use of technical
terms. He is obligated, as a scientist, to carefully define his terms
and to use them consistently thereafter in his work. Such
consistency is particularly relevant in theorizing. There are various
ways of designating the classes of terms used in theory work.
Selected examples will help to illustrate the point. Brodbeck said:

> A theory contains two classes of descriptive terms: basic or "primitive,"
> and defined. The basic terms of a theory are those that are not them-
> selves defined within the theory, but all other descriptive terms of the
> theory are defined by means of them. The basic terms of a theory must
> occur in its axioms and may also reoccur in its theorems. Its defined
> terms occur only in the theorems.[14]

Under the subject of "theoretical terms," Kaplan specified
observation terms, indirect observable terms, constructs, and
theoretical terms. However, he indicated little consistency in use of
this nomenclature and ended his discussion by noting that there
really are no differences among the discriminations.[15] Gordon and
others divided theory into three main classes: primitive terms, key
terms, and theoretical terms.[16] Primitive terms cannot be

---

[14]*Op. cit.*, p. 70.

[15]Abraham Kaplan, *The Conduct of Inquiry* (San Francisco: Chandler Publishing Company, 1964), pp.
54-60.

[16]Ira J. Gordon, Chairman, "Theories of Instruction: A Set of Guidelines," a position paper
prepared by the Commission on Instructional Theory and presented at the Annual Conference of the
Association for Supervision and Curriculum Development, NEA at Dallas, Texas in March, 1967.

operationally defined; they maintain a constant meaning. The concept *point* in geometry is a good example. Key terms are those which must be operationally defined such as *reinforcement* or *problem solving*. Theoretical terms are operationally defined but in relationship with key terms. *Motivation* and *set* are examples. Sophisticated theories will contain all three types of terms.

Despite the various ways of designating classes of terms, the theorist probably should be aware of at least three classes he might be called upon to choose and use. They may be called general language terms, basic concepts, and theoretical constructs. The first are those terms that are used in science and in general language in common. These are the words that make the sentences of a theory such as many of the verbs and adjectives. It is not necessary that they be defined at all, much less operationally defined, because their use has become commonly accepted. A second group consists of those concepts that are basic to the set of events being explained. These are well-defined constructs, and they are usually operationally defined. Such terms as *molecule* in chemistry, *mass* in physics, or *curriculum* in education would fit in this category. A third group consists of those that are essential to the theory. These words have meaning for the system of events being encompassed by the theory, but they cannot be identified by direct observation. Such terms as *emotional need*, *persecution complex*, or *attitude* belong in this category.

Statements

A theory, by definition, contains a set of statements within which terms are used. The statements themselves fall into different classes just as the terms do. Statements are referred to differentially as facts, definitions, propositions, hypotheses, generalizations, axioms, postulates, theorems, assumptions, and laws. Sometimes these referents are used interchangeably and in slightly varying contexts, and some of them are more or less self-explanatory. But for purposes of remaining clear as to their use in this text, even the more self-evident will be defined.

A fact is a phenomenon known by observation. A definition is a formal statement of meaning or signification. A proposition is a formal statement affirming or denying something about a subject.

Hypotheses, generalizations, axioms, postulates, theorems, and laws are special cases of the proposition. An hypothesis consists of one or more propositions designed to explain a set of events. A generalization is a proposition which makes an assertion about one or more members of a class; it is derived by inference from observed relationships. An axiom, or a postulate, is a proposition assumed to be true. A theorem is a proposition derived by reasoning or deduced from axioms. A law is a proposition that remains invariable given unchanging conditions. In essence, it is a generalization accepted by the scientific community. An assumption is a conjecture, or supposition, that may take the form of an axiom, postulate, theorem or hypothesis. It helps the theorist to look at theory statements in the light of the functions expected of theories.

FUNCTIONS OF THEORY

Our understanding of the meaning of theory may be augmented if we note some of the functions associated with theory. The range of these is very broad, but at the same time they lack cohesiveness. Theorists may exhibit different focal points for their efforts, but at the same time there is general agreement among scientists and philosophers of science that ". . . theories fulfill the three functions of, (1) description, (2) prediction, and (3) explanation."[17] These functions bear upon the theory that the scientist tries to understand, and they have implications for persons who may be using theories. Gowin acknowledged the latter when he said:

> But turn theory around and point it toward the person using the theory. A different set of functions seems to be prominent when we look at the theorist at work in research. Here the theory helps the researcher to *analyze* data, to make a short-hand summarization or *synopsis* of data and relations, and to *suggest* new things to try out. Theory functions in analysis, in synopsis, in power of suggestion or speculation. Theory functions as something to think with, to help in one's work.[18]

Probably the most simple function of a theory is to provide a system for classifying the knowledge of that theoretical field.

---

[17]O'Connor, *op. cit.*, p. 81.

[18]D.B. Gowin, "Can Educational Theory Guide Practice?" *Educational Theory,* 13:8, January, 1963.

Homans has expressed this function in the following picturesque way:

> Even the most fragile theory has its uses. In its lowest form, as a classification, it provides a set of pigeonholes, a filing cabinet, in which fact can accumulate. . . . In time the accumulation makes necessary a more economical filing system, with more cross references, and a new theory is born.[19]

The ordering of facts and observations into some scheme is fundamental to description of any field about which theorizing is to be done. It is a way of arranging information so that the scope and the internal relationships of the total body of information is more visible. As Brodbeck stated: "A theory not only explains and predicts, it also unifies phenomena."[20]

At a higher level, those functions are added that permit moving beyond classification or collection of facts to action of broader scope such as that involved in induction and prediction. Whereas it is true that the ordering of information in a systematic manner is a task of theorizing, the task really is but a prelude to the fulfillment of the larger functions of theory. With these being description, prediction, and explanation, theory building reaches its most systematic level when the resulting theory becomes a full-blown logico-deductive system, or a logico-mathematical system. These high-level goals are reached most easily in the natural sciences, but in the social sciences the complications of the sets of events to be explained by theories may force theorists to temporarily lesser levels of achievement. Very few theoretical systems utilizing symbols and mathematical structures have been created in the social sciences. Instead, verbal models are used extensively as ways of representing particular phenomena. Nevertheless, theories in the social sciences must meet the basic criteria for theorizing and these include the organization of relationships so that they are better explained and so that predictions can be made for events not yet observed from known relationships.

We return for a moment to Kerlinger's definition which illustrates the three theory functions of description, prediction, and explanation. First, the definition calls for description through

---

[19]George Homans, *The Human Group* (New York: Harcourt, Brace and World, Inc., 1950), p. 5.
[20]*Op. cit.*, p. 70.

the character of the propositions offered and the delineated relationships among the propositions and constructs. By studying what variables are related and how they are related, the researcher is able to develop predictable relationships between certain variables. All of these explain the set of events.

It has been emphasized that a main purpose of theories is to explain selected phenomena or events. The idea of explanation is interpretable two ways. One is to give an account of something; the other is to account for something.[21] This distinction is an interesting one because it relates to the levels of theorizing described in the foregoing paragraphs. Very often those who become involved in classification as a theorizing activity are working at the task of giving an account of something; whereas, the individual who builds a predictive system is accounting for something through the established predictable relationships. It is one thing to give an anecdotal account of the daily behavior of an aggressive child in a school classroom, but another to relate that meaningfully to the phenomenon of prediction.

It could be said that in his drive to describe, explain, and predict, the theorist is striving to work himself out of business, for he is constantly deriving new laws and seeking new relationships among the laws expressed by the theory. One might think that within a given set of events all of the laws and their interrelationships could be stated and the theory itself thereby become a higher law. However, the theorist is never satisfied with that condition if it ever occurs. He then seeks out new relationships by combining sets of events into a new universal set and then proceeding with the search for new relationships and new laws in a new theory. Kaplan expressed this heuristic function of theory when he stated: "What is important is that laws propagate when they are united in a theory: theory serves as matchmaker, midwife, and godfather all in one."[22] The great advances in the sciences are made by theory building more than through empiricism because of this generative function of theorizing.

---

[21] This distinction was made by Herbert Feigl in a speech given at a colloquium at Northwestern University in January 1966. Feigl holds that the latter is the task of theory.

[22] *Op. cit.*, p. 303.

PROCESSES IN THEORY BUILDING

More insight into theory and its processes is possible by examining selected tasks performed by the theorist. Two things stand out glaringly. One is that the range of activity is large. The second is that working rules tend to be dictated more by the choice of activity than by any arbitrary set of rules for theory building. These points may be amplified by an examination of some of the suggestions that have been made.

The language used in theory building is a matter of concern as exemplified by the attention currently being given to discovery and delineation of concepts and to the problems of definition of terms. For example, Homans listed the following rules for theory builders, most of which have to do with problems of communicating:

> Look first at the obvious, the familiar, the common. In a science that has not established its foundations, these are the things that best repay study.
>
> State the obvious in its full generality. Science is an economy of thought only if its hypotheses sum up in a simple form a large number of facts.
>
> Talk about one thing at a time. That is, in choosing your words, (or more pedantically, concepts) see that they refer not to several classes of fact at the same time but to one and to one only. Corollary: Once you have chosen your words, always use the same words when referring to the same thing.
>
> Cut down as far as you dare the number of things you are talking about. "As few as you may; as many as you must," is the rule governing the number of classes of fact you take into account.
>
> Once you have started to talk, do not stop until you have finished. That is, describe systematically the relationships between the facts designated by your words.
>
> Recognize that your analysis must be abstract, because it deals with only a few elements of the concrete situation. Admit the dangers of abstraction, especially when action is required, but do not be afraid of abstraction.[23]

Mouly identified the following four characteristics of a good theory which have implications for theory-building activities:

---

[23]*Op. cit.*, pp. 6-17.

1.   A theoretical system must permit deductions which can be tested empirically — i.e., it must provide the means for its own interpretation and verification. . . .

2.   Theory must be compatible both with observation and with previously validated theories. . . .

3.   Theories must be stated in simple terms; that theory is best which explains the most in the simplest form. . . .

4.   Scientific theories must be based on empirical facts and relationships.[24]

More specifically, curriculum theorists need to think in terms of the precise activities they perform when working at theorizing. One such activity is the formulation of definitions. A second is the classification of relevant information into homogeneous categories. A third is the utilization of the inductive and deductive processes. A fourth, and very important one, is the making of inferences and predictions and the testing of them in the crucible of research. A fifth is the development of models. A sixth is sub-theory formation. All six of these principal theory-building activities are crucial; therefore, each of them will be discussed more fully in the following pages.

Definition of Terms

Description of theory, rules laid down by Homans, and the characteristics described by Mouly, all carry the emphatic message that careful definition of terms is an essential ingredient in the work of a theorist. Two rules seem to govern the activity of definition. One is clarity of wording to assure exact meaning; the other is consistency in use of terms once they have been defined. The terms or constructs of any area of scientific endeavor are the subject matter of that area. The technical terms or constructs of physics and biology, for instance, distinguish between the two sciences. They are the tools for thinking and communicating.

If the reader were to review any significant portion of the literature discussing kinds of definitions and rules for making them, he would find a plethora of names attributed to different kinds of definitions and different kinds of terms or concepts. The

[24]George J. Mouly, *The Science of Educational Research* (2d ed.; New York: American Book Company, 1970), pp. 70-71.

terms that the theorist is most likely to be concerned with are general terms, basic concepts, and theoretical terms. For purposes of establishing definitions, the theorists would be concerned primarily with the basic and theoretical terms. It should be kept in mind here that the basic terms are axiomatically defined while the theoretical terms must be operationally defined.

Brodbeck distinguished between nominal and operational definitions.[25] Nominal definitions give the attributes associated with the term or concept. In this way a term is explained by listing the boundaries of interpretation. Operational definitions, on the other hand, are more complicated in that the conditions under which a concept is used are a part of the definition. The operational definition assumes an "if-then" condition, meaning that if certain conditions exist, then the statement within which the term is used is true. Or, a term is recognized if prescribed conditions exist. When a term is a theoretical term, the concept usually is called an operational construct.

There seems to be universal agreement that definition of technical terms is an important and a critical activity for the theorist. Two reasons predominate. The selection and definition of terms or concepts aid in defining the subject matter boundaries for the theorist's work, and the consistent use of the defined terms facilitates explanation and prediction.

Classification

Classification is another theory-building activity. It is reiterated here that Homans referred to classification as the lowest form of theory, but he pointed out the possibility of a classification system becoming or producing new theory. Classification, however, need not always be thought of as a simple pigeonholing activity. Hall and Lindzey suggested that one of the functions of a theory is to incorporate known findings into a consistent and reasonable framework.[26] In this sense, classification as a theory-building activity becomes a means of organizing and integrating what is known about the areas in which the theorizing activity is being conducted. Through classification, it is possible for

---

[25]*Op. cit.*, pp. 48-51.
[26]Hall and Lindzey, *op. cit.*, p. 13.

the classifier to become aware of the voids in knowledge necessary to give meaning to a given activity or series of events. It is the function of research to fill these gaps. The observation of relationships among classified elements can be included as part of the classification activity.

Sometimes a developed classification scheme, or a taxonomy, actually is called a theory. Such designation is often misleading because a classification scheme cannot fulfill all of the requisites of a theory. Classification as a theorizing activity helps to group facts and generalizations into homogeneous groups, but it does not explain the interrelationships among the groups or the relationships among the facts and generalizations within any single group. In a sense, developing a classification scheme is a terminal activity. A theory, on the other hand, fosters new relationships and conditions for understanding. Nonetheless, the development of classification schemes is a theorizing activity, even though it may be done in the early stages of theory development.

Induction and Deduction

Induction and deduction are the two basic processes for generating theoretical statements beyond those of definition of terms and arrangement of classification schemes. Induction is a process whereby a larger generalization is derived from a set of facts of more limited scope. By so doing, the inductive argument allows the theorizer to extend the range of his knowledge. For example, a person notes that all dogs he has observed have had a liver, and he concludes that all dogs have livers. His conclusion contains information not present in his premise, and the conclusion is probably true, but not necessarily true, if the premise is true. In a sense, a generalization arrived at through research has an inductive relation to the evidence supporting the generalization.

Deduction is a process whereby a conclusion is reached that is entirely conclusive or entirely inconclusive. The conclusion is restricted by the premises of the argument. For example, if we observe that every mammal has a liver and that all dogs are mammals, we may conclude that every dog has a liver. Thus, the deductive argument makes explicit the content of the premises of the argument.

From the definitions of theory given earlier in the chapter, it can be seen that different kinds of theory are produced by the inductive and the deductive processes. The inductive process tends to produce normative or prescriptive types of theory; whereas, the deductive process tends to produce logico-deductive types of theory. Since both prescriptive and deductive statements normally are used at one stage or another in the development of theories in the social sciences, it would be an error to say that one of the two processes is preferential. Both processes are implicitly or directly demanded by the definitions of theory and the theory-building processes discussed thus far, but induction and deduction become critical when one thinks about inference, prediction, and research as theory processes.

Inference, Prediction, Research

A complex of theory-building activities may be included under the process of inference. In general, the act of inferring means to go beyond the known or the observed. More specifically, the activities may include making assumptions, deriving hypotheses, reaching generalizations from observations, and deducing from observations and generalizations.

A theorist is forced to make assumptions because, by definition of theory, he is faced with the problem of explaining the character of and the relationships among events that are both known and unknown. For example, he may assume the nature of theoretical constructs, or he may assume axiomatic conditions. He may assume pertinence of additional facts or cause and effect relationships among various events within the total set of events. He may make any of these assumptions for purposes of establishing continuity or meaning in his theory, or he may make them for operational purposes in a research program.

The use of the hypothesis in theory building is as clear as it is in research. It is a testable supposition about relations among identified phenomena; it is simply a device for verifying a stated assumption so as to reach a conclusion. From repeated use of the hypothesis, the theory builder can formulate postulates, theorems, or laws governing the interrelationships of his theory elements.

The two additional activities mentioned above as related to the process of inference are generalization and deduction. These were somewhat discussed earlier under induction and deduction as primary theory-building processes. Repeatedly, a theorist observes events and then generalizes from related or similar results. Some generalizations are reached by concluding from the acceptance of premises considered to be true. Scientific generalizations, however, are induced from supporting evidence. Deduction produces generalizations, or conclusions, that must be completely true so long as the evidence leading to the conclusion are valid evidence. A theorist concludes from a series of generalizations a law or theorem in which he has great confidence.

There is no question but that some of the terms included here under the concept of inference are used interchangeably or synonymously in the literature. They reveal the variety of processes that the theory builder has at his command to do his work. The main point of inference as a theory-building activity is that one must go beyond the simple observation and classification of observations if a working theory is to be built.

It is stated repeatedly in the literature that the real test of a theory is the reliability of the prediction that can be made from it. The principal function of a theory is to give greater meaning to a set of events; the greater meaning would involve both what is known about the set of events from observations already made and the unknown expressed through inference of some sort. Events associated with a practice that is perpetuated have greater meaning, in spite of the unknown, because a theory provides a rationale for their existence. In learning theory, for example, the phenomenon of transfer of training must be accounted for to explain certain kinds of learning behavior. Both facts and inference must be posed by the learning theorist before transfer of training can become a useful concept in his theory. But the real test of the theorist's structure of the transfer of training concept comes when transfer effect is predicted by means of the theory in a behavioral situation, and the prediction is subsequently tested. The struggle for prediction in theory was uniquely expressed by Bales:

> As a predictor, the scientific theorizer, like the practical human being he is theorizing about, has to reduce his demands for an omniscient information-gathering apparatus if he wants to predict forward in real time from real information. The trick in improving prediction, since omniscience is so hard to come by, must lie in learning how to get more

information or how to make more and better inferences from what we have, or both, and to do either or both before something else happens. These are the requirements of naturalistic prediction, and all good theory must eventually face up to them. But as a theorizer, the scientific predictor, like the theorizing human being he is predicting about, has to be prepared to think and talk about states of affairs to which he has had no empirical access, as he struggles by symbolic means to construct an omniscient perspective.[27]

There is a reciprocal relation between research and theory building. A theory builder must conduct research and the results of research contribute to theory development. Particularly in its early states of development, a theory consists of statements that are assumptive or tentative as part of the explanation of the set of events. It also would consist of statements covering events or conditions that belong in the category of the known. Research builds upon what is known by probing from there into what is unknown. Similarly, research procedures are used to move the more tentative generalizations toward the status of laws. The reciprocal relationship lies in the fact that the theory-building tasks drive the theorist into research and control the character of his research. This interaction phenomenon between theory and research is what produces the most systematic research programs which, in turn, produce more valid theories.

Inference, prediction, and research are the activities that really distinguish the work of the theorist. They result in the creating of laws and the identifying of relationships among the laws. Implied in these processes is a movement from hunch, or assumption, to generalization based on some evidence (postulates), to deductions from the postulates, to hypotheses to be researched for purposes of stating laws that improve explanation of the set of events. The quality of theorizing is a function of the precision with which the theorist uses these processes.

Model Building

Model building is a frequently used process in theorizing. Models are analogies. The construction of a model is a way of representing given phenomena and their relationships, but they

---

[27]Robert F. Bales, "Small-Group Theory Research," *Sociology Today*, edited by Robert K. Merton, Leonard Broom, and Leonard S. Cottrell, Jr. (New York: Basic Books, Inc., 1959), p. 297.

are not phenomena. For example, a model of an ocean liner is not the ocean liner. A set of blueprints is not a house. Functionally, models are used to represent events and event interactions in a highly compact and illustrative manner. So employed, they help to explain facts or events that are puzzling. Thus, they are an aid in theory building.

Parenthetically, we should mention the word "paradigm," for there appears to be considerable uncertainty as to its meaning. At one extreme it is used as a synonym for model. At the other is the very complicated and broad use as uniquely employed by Kuhn. Kuhn suggested ". . . that some accepted examples of actual scientific practice — examples which include law, theory, application, and instrumentation together — provide models from which spring particular coherent traditions of scientific research."[28] Thus, Kuhn uses the paradigm as an example shared by members of the community of science from one generation to another and from the development of one scientific field to another. To point up a major distinction between a paradigm and a model we might say that a paradigm is a framework borrowed from its field of origin and subsequently used in a different field of endeavor; whereas, a model is a representation of a specific set of events about which a theory is being developed.

Now, let us return to our discussion of model building as a device in theorizing. A basic purpose for developing models was implied by Rivett when he defined a model as ". . . a set of logical relationships, either qualitative or quantitative, which will link together the relevant features of the reality with which we are concerned."[29] Thus conceived, the model is a device to help the theorist identify his events and to show the relationships among them. Kaplan was more specific when he distinguished the following different senses in which the term "model" is used:

> (1) any theory more strictly formulated than is characteristic of the literary, academic, or eristic cognitive styles, one presented with some degree of mathematical exactness and logical rigor; (2) a semantical model, presenting a conceptual analogue to some subject-matter; (3) a physical model, a nonlinguistic system analogous to some other being

---

[28]Thomas S. Kuhn, *The Structure of Scientific Revolutions* (2d ed., enl.; Chicago: The University of Chicago Press, 1970), p. 10.

[29]Patrick Rivett, *Principles of Model Building* (New York: John Wiley & Sons, 1972), p. 9.

studied; (4) a formal model, a model *of* a theory which presents the latter purely as a structure of uninterpreted symbols; (5) an interpretive model, providing an interpretation *for* a formal theory.[30]

Brodbeck claimed two major uses of the term. On the one hand, a model, she said, is used for highly speculative or quantified theories. On the other hand, the set of laws for one theory can be used as a model for another when the laws of the two are of the same form or isomorphic.[31] In spite of the labels put on various forms or kinds of models, they basically are either replicas of a set of laws or events, or they represent the set of laws or events symbolically. A good point was made by O'Connor when he wrote:

> Thus models in science act like metaphors in language; they enlighten us by suggesting arguments by analogy from known resemblances to resemblances so far unnoticed. They may also act as aids to the type of explanation discussed below. But by themselves, they are no more than a useful stimulus to the process of explanation.[32]

In theorizing, models can serve several functions. Fattu depicted them as providing ways of representation, rules of inference, interpretation, and visualization.[33] Models are useful tools, and theorists make extensive use of them. Like the classification scheme, however, the model is not the theory. The person developing a theory cannot be satisfied with modeling except as a means to an end.

Sub-theory Formation

One of the things that characterizes a mature and comprehensive theory is the development of sub-theories. Sub-theories tend to broaden the scope of a theory as well as to improve the total explanation of the sets of events involved. However, one should not confuse the development of competing theories in a given area with the development of sub-theories in any one theory. For example, it is one thing to talk about the development of learning theories in psychology such as those of

---

[30]*Op. cit.*, pp. 267-68.

[31]*Op. cit.*, pp. 88-93.

[32]*Op. cit.*, p. 90.

[33]N.A. Fattu, "A Model of Teaching as Problem Solving," *Theories of Instruction*, edited by James B. Macdonald and Robert R. Leeper (Washington: the Association for Supervision and Curriculum Development, NEA, 1965), pp. 63-64.

Thorndike, Hull, Tolman, or Levin. It is quite another for any single theory to be distinguished by its unique sub-theories in regard to such issues as transfer, motivation, verbal learning, or retention.

SUMMARY

The purpose of this chapter was to present the meaning and consequences of theory building. The following paragraphs seem to be warranted conclusions.

Theory is defined in several ways. There is general agreement that a theory is a set of statements explaining some series of events. Variations in definition are due to the character of the statement and the kind of event relevant to the theory.

The primary functions of theories are description, prediction, and explanation. These functions are both demanding upon and of service to the theorist. They demand the vigor of description and explanation, and at the same time, they serve as a directive force for the theorist's work.

A theory is composed of a set of statements. Essential to the statements are the terms that define the subject matter of the area. In addition to the commonly used terms that have accepted meanings, there are the terms that are basic to the set of events being explained and the essential theoretical terms. Statements of a theory within which the terms are used may be expressed in such forms as statements of fact, definitions, propositions, postulates, hypotheses, deductions, assumptions, generalizations, laws, axioms, or theorems.

The processes of theorizing can be pinpointed further by identifying some of the tasks for people concerned with theory building. As in all scientific work, the careful definition of technical terms and constructs is one important task. Another is the classification of known and assumed information. Probably the most critical and unique tasks in theorizing are the making and testing of inferences and predictions. Two additional activities are the development of models and sub-theories.

The work of the theorist is broad in scope and intensity. Few people will perform at all possible levels. The uninitiated may begin with some limited task, but it is predictable that his work will broaden at every turn.

Finally, I should like to emphasize that there are three primary rules to which anyone who wishes to engage in theory building must adhere. A first rule is to discipline one's use of technical terms. There are two dimensions of this rule. One is to clarify wording to transmit exact meaning, and the other is to consistently use terms throughout the theoretical work. Any theorist is obligated to carefully define his basic and theoretical terms and to be consistent in their use thereafter for these are the primary mechanisms whereby he directs his own procedures and disciplines the communication of his works to others. A second rule is to identify the principle ingredients, i.e., the subjects and processes, that are essential to the theory. To do so it is necessary to arrange in some logical order the knowledge, the key concepts, the assumptions, and the propositions associated with the set of events under study. When a theorist follows this rule, he goes beyond definition and boxes in his whole field of concern. Essentially, classification is the process here. A third rule is to describe and explain relationships among the various parts of the theoretical statements and to explain the character of those relationships. Most theories are complex wholes. The various parts may have individual meaning or significance, but meaning and significance are enhanced as the parts are related to the whole. Logic and research are the primary mechanisms for implementing this rule.

SUGGESTED READINGS

Abel, Theodore. "The Present Status of Social Theory," *American Sociological Review,* 17:156-167, April, 1952.

Bales, Robert F. "Small-Group Theory and Research," *Sociology Today.* Robert K. Merton, Leonard Broom, and Leonard S. Cottrell, Jr., editors. New York: Basic Books, Inc., 1959, pp. 293-305.

Blalock, Hubert M., Jr. *Theory Construction From Verbal to Mathematical Foundations.* Englewood Cliffs, N.J.: Prentice-Hall, Inc., 1969.

Braithwaite, Richard B. *Scientific Explanation.* New York: Harper and Row, 1960.

Brodbeck, May. "Logic and Scientific Method in Research on Teaching," *Handbook of Research on Teaching,* N.L. Gage, editor. Chicago: Rand McNally and Company, 1963, pp. 44-93.

Brodbeck, May. "Models, Meaning and Theories," *Symposium on Sociological Theory,* Llewellyn Gross, editor. Evanston: Row Peterson and Company, 1959, pp. 373-403.

Brody, Baruch A. *Readings in the Philosophy of Science*. Englewood Cliffs, N.J.: Prentice-Hall, Inc., 1970.

Conant, James B. *Modern Science and Modern Man*. Garden City, N.J.: Doubleday and Company, Inc., 1952.

Dubin, Robert. *Theory Building*. New York: The Free Press, 1969.

Feigl, Herbert. "Principles and Problems of Theory Construction in Psychology," *Current Trends in Psychological Theory*. Pittsburgh: University of Pittsburgh Press, 1951, pp. 179-213.

Galtung, Johan. *Theory and Methods of Social Research*. New York: Columbia University Press, 1967.

Gowin, D.B. "Can Educational Theory Guide Practice?" *Educational Theory*, 13:6-12, January, 1963.

Hempel, Carl G. *Philosophy of Natural Science*. Englewood Cliffs, N.J.: Prentice-Hall, Inc., 1966.

Homans, George. *The Human Group*. New York: Harcourt, Brace and World, Inc., 1950.

Kaplan, Abraham. *The Conduct of Inquiry*. San Francisco: Chandler Publishing Company, 1964.

Kerlinger, Fred N. *Foundations of Behavioral Research*. 2d ed. New York: Holt, Rinehart, and Winston, Inc., 1973.

Kuhn, Thomas S. *The Structure of Scientific Revolutions*. 2d ed. Chicago: University of Chicago Press, 1970.

Logan, Frank and David Olmstead. *Behavior Theory and Social Science*. New Haven: Yale University Press, 1955.

Marx, Melvin H. (ed.). *Theories in Contemporary Psychology*. New York: The Macmillan Company, 1963.

Merton, Robert K. *Social Theory and Social Structure*. New York: The Free Press, 1968.

Morgenbesser, Sidney (ed.). *Philosophy of Science Today*. New York: Basic Books, Inc., 1967.

O'Connor, D.J. *An Introduction to the Philosophy of Education*. London: Routledge and Kegan Paul, 1957.

Parsons, Talcott and Edward A. Shils (eds.). *Foundations of Modern Sociological Theory*. Glencoe, Ill.: The Free Press, 1961.

Parsons, Talcott. "General Theory in Sociology," *Sociology Today*. Robert K. Merton, Leonard Broom, and Leonard S. Cottrell, Jr., editors. New York: Basic Books, Inc., 1959, pp. 3-38.

Prior, Moody E. *Science and the Humanities*. Evanston: Northwestern University Press, 1962.

Rivett, Patrick. *Principles of Model Building*. New York: John Wiley and Sons, 1972.

Rose, Arnold M. "Generalizations in the Social Sciences," *American Journal of Sociology*, 59:49-58, July, 1953.

Rose, Arnold M. *Theory and Method in the Social Sciences*. Minneapolis: University of Minnesota Press, 1954.

Rudner, Richard S. *Philosophy of Social Science*. Englewood Cliffs, N.J.: Prentice-Hall, Inc., 1966.

Snow, Richard E. "Theory Construction for Research on Teaching," *Second Handbook of Research on Teaching*, Robert M. W. Travers, editor. Chicago: Rand McNally & Company, 1973, pp. 77-112.

Toulmin, Stephen. *The Philosophy of Science*. New York: Harper and Row, 1960.

Travers, Robert M.W. *An Introduction to Educational Research*. 3rd ed. New York: The Macmillan Company, 1969.

Turner, M.B. *Philosophy and the Science of Behavior*. New York: Appleton-Century-Crofts, Inc., 1967.

Whitehead, Alfred North. *Science and the Modern World*. New York: The Free Press, 1925.

Zetterberg, Hans L. *On Theory and Verification in Sociology*. 3rd ed. Totowa, N.J.: The Bedminster Press, 1965.

Chapter 3

THEORY IN EDUCATION

Against this background of general information about the processes of theorizing, we turn now to an examination of the kinds of theorizing done within the broad field of education. The purpose of a chapter on educational theory at this point is to serve as a link between the foregoing discussion of theory building and a discussion of the problems involved in curriculum theory development. If the reader will refer again to Figure 1, page 5, he will observe educational theory to be an applied theory and an outgrowth of developments in theories in the basic disciplines. This means that many of the problems for educational theory stem from practice. Since education is an applied discipline, educational theories technically are not sub-theories to theories in the basic disciplines. But beginning with theories in education in Figure 1, heavy lines have been drawn to indicate that curriculum theories are sub-theories to educational theories, and the theories indicated on the bottom line are sub-theories to curriculum theories. In fact, the order of events in Figure 1 is the rationale for the chapter organization of this book. Our discussion is organized to begin with a search for rules for theory building among the established disciplines, to move to theory development in education, and finally to substantial consideration of curriculum theory. In this chapter, we are concerned with thinking and developments in educational theory.

Traditionally, the word "theory" has been employed in educational literature without definition. For example, in the otherwise carefully prepared publication, the *Encyclopedia of Educational Research*, neither "theory" nor "educational theory" was indexed, much less defined. There are two possible explanations for the omission. One is that the dimensions of educational theory had not been defined carefully enough for the topics to be discussed in an orderly fashion. A second is that there was not sufficient research on the subject to warrant its treatment in an encyclopedia devoted exclusively to research. In discussing the status of educational theory as of 1959, Bayles claimed that educational theory in the United States seemed to be in "a state of suspended animation." In his opinion, assumptions about the social context of education need to be clarified before a sound theoretical structure can be built.[1] A decade later Travers labeled the theories used in educational research as generalizations, but generalizations without the certainty, usefulness, or status of law.[2] On a more general level, Sizer registered frustration over "the persistent unwillingness of many professional educators to respect and use theory."[3] These comments illustrate the failure of scholars in education to introduce the rigors of sound theory building to the sets of events attributable to the field of education.

Despite these apparent shortcomings, theory in education has been a topic of serious discussion for a number of years, and in recent ones, the procedures of the natural and social scientist applied to the description and explanation of educational phenomena have opened up new vistas. A reasonable prediction is that educational theory will grow, but it will grow first from the sub-theories now being developed within the broad field of education.

Quite obviously, it is beyond the scope of this writing to review the entire history of the use of the concept "theory" in education or to review the nature of all so-called educational theories. It is possible, however, to relate the meaning and use of theory in related disciplines to its meaning and use in education. In this chapter, we will discuss the global aspects of educational theory and follow that with a review of exemplar sub-theory developments in school administration and instruction. Curriculum theory as a

---

[1]Ernest Bayles, "Present Status of Educational Theory in the U.S." *School and Society*, 87:5-7, January, 1959.

[2]Robert M.W. Travers, *An Introduction to Educational Research* (3rd ed.; New York: The Macmillan Company, 1969), p. 21.

[3]Theodore Sizer, "Commentary: Three Major Frustrations: Ruminations of a Retiring Dean," *National Elementary Principal*, 52:74, January, 1973.

third sub-theory of education will then be our concern for the remainder of the book.

APPROACHES TO EDUCATIONAL THEORY

Even a casual review of literature discussing theory in education indicates great disparity among the approaches made. For the most part, each approach is a direct function of the frame of reference of the author. For example, the hard-nosed practitioner may pose the world of theory in education as a hindrance to progress in the practice of running schools. A philosopher may equate philosophy with theory. A person who is seriously attempting to develop the field of educational theory utilizing the techniques of philosophy and science will assume a more global posture.

Theory and Practice

The notion that theoretical work in education is antithetical to the world of practice is frequently stipulated. Educational literature contains abundant discourse on the subject of the relationships between theory and practice. Unfortunately, most of it takes a negative instead of a positive approach. The point of view is that theory is something to be tolerated in small quantities at the college or university level, but it is to be forgotten or downgraded by school administrators and classroom teachers, who are expected to be "practical" people. Such comments are not based upon a careful consideration of the relationships that need to exist between theory and practice if either is to be consistent and constructive.

To some extent, confusion is multiplied by failure of commentators to discriminate between research that contributes to the formation of laws pertaining to explanation and prediction, and research applied to field situations which are not necessarily related to any larger series of events. Theory by its very nature is impractical. The world of practicality is built around clusters of specific events. The world of theory derives from generalizations, laws, axioms, and theorems explaining specific events and the relationships among them.

The fact that the worlds of theory and practice are different does not minimize the known interrelationships that exist between them. The operational vistas opened up and explained by theories increase the possible choices of behaving for the practitioner; the theories, however, do not tell him how to act. A theory may clarify relationships among any given set of events, but it does not and cannot direct the execution of that set of events. Newsome made this distinction clear when he noted that theory is not what is practiced.[4] A person cannot practice a set of logically related statements; he performs an activity. Theories of instruction, for example, might account for classroom discipline, grouping practices, lesson planning, and instructional materials as components of instruction, but the theories cannot tell teachers how to behave with respect to those functions. Conversely, empirical information may be accumulated as a result of practices in schooling, but the accumulated data will not in itself explain or predict similar events elsewhere. Nevertheless, as Gowin put it, ". . . it is the job of educational theory to guide educational practices."[5] In turn, theory is modified by practice and research that emanates from it. We will have more to say about the relationship between theory and practices in education in the subsequent discussion of the more global developments in educational theory.

Theory and Philosophy in Education

It is to be expected that educational literature reveals a very close relationship between philosophy of education and educational theory. This relationship highlights the conflict in some educational circles between a scientific approach to the development of theory and a more prescriptive approach. It is convenient to say that there are two basic kinds of theory — prescriptive theory and descriptive theory. It is also a convenience to relate descriptive theory development with the scientific approach and prescriptive theory development with the techniques of philosophy. As indicated in Chapter 2, descriptive theories normally consist of a set of propositions that are logically interrelated from which relationships may be demonstrated and

[4]George L. Newsome, Jr. "In What Sense is Theory a Guide to Practice in Education?" *Educational Theory*, 14:36, January, 1964.

[5]D.B. Gowin, "Can Educational Theory Guide Practice?" *Educational Theory*, 13:8, January, 1963.

new information derived by deductive processes. Prescriptive theories, on the other hand, consist of a set of proposals for action or a set of propositions about a body of related problems. It is in the realm of prescriptive theory that philosophy exerts its influence.

The closeness of the provinces of philosophy and theory was illustrated by Dewey in the statement:

> If we are willing to conceive education as the process of forming fundamental dispositions, intellectual and emotional, toward nature and fellow men, philosophy may even be defined *as the general theory of education*.[6]

If one accepts the above conclusion, it becomes obvious that many theories must be developed within the general area of philosophy to account for the many dimensions of education and for differing basic philosophies. For example, a good philosophy must encompass a theory of knowledge. Comparably, a philosophy of education should lead to the formulation of a theory of method. Values and ethics, both in the purview of philosophy, play a significant role in education. Because of these reciprocal concerns, philosophy has a close relationship to theory development in education.

Various philosophies of education have been posed as theories of education. In an issue of *School and Society* devoted to educational theories, several different theories based upon philosophical positions were analyzed. Broudy espoused the cause of realism.[7] Butler defended modern idealism.[8] McMurray identified and elaborated the status of pragmatism in education.[9] Brameld, as would be expected, went to the defense of reconstructionism.[10] Pratte similarly associated philosophical positions with educational theories when he identified as contemporary theories of education: Progressive Education I (natural selection), Progressive Education II (experimentalism), essentialism, perennialism, reconstructionism, and existentialism.[11] Each of these positions is

---

[6]John Dewey, *Democracy and Education* (New York: The Macmillan Company, 1916), p. 383.

[7]Harry S. Broudy, "Realism in American Education," *School and Society*, 87:11-14, January 17, 1959.

[8]J. Donald Butler, "Idealism in Education Today," *School and Society*, 87:8-10, January 17, 1959.

[9]Foster McMurray, "The Present Status of Pragmatism in Education," *School and Society*, 87:14-18, January 17, 1959.

[10]Theodore Brameld, "Imperatives for a Reconstructed Philosophy of Education," *School and Society*, 87:18-20, January 17, 1959.

[11]Richard Pratte, *Contemporary Theories of Education* (Scranton, Pa.: Intext Educational Publishers, 1971).

dictated by philosophical attitudes toward the role of the school, the nature of knowledge, the nature and derivation of values, and the nature of man. All of these latter impinge on the education function.

In analyzing confusion and conflict in educational theory, Black labeled four theories: Traditionalist, Progressive, the Learning-Product Theory, and the Learning-Process Theory. The Traditionalist adherents were identified with the transmission of the cultural heritage as the role of the school in the manner of the pre-Rousseau period. The Progressive adherents looked to such persons as Johann Herbart, Charles Judd, H.C. Morrison, and F.W. Parker for a point of view. The emphasis was on transmission of the social heritage which took the individual into account. The Learning-Process adherents were associated with such persons as Rousseau, Pestalozzi, Froebel, William James, G. Stanley Hall, John Dewey, William Kilpatrick, John Childs, Boyd Bode, and Harold Rugg. They emphasized the individual but recognized the school's role in the transmission of cultural heritage.[12] In 1966, Black restated his viewpoints on the same subject. Again he placed in polar positions Extreme Progressivism and Extreme Traditionalism with Learning-Process Theory and the Learning-Product Theory interposed between them. He stated:

> This four-fold classificatory scheme thus recognizes four aspects of education and distinguishes the four classes of educational theories according to differences in emphasis. Four concepts — education as transmission of the social heritage, education as individual development, education as a product, and education as a process — are the differentiating factors.[13]

Black concluded by averring that present-day philosophers lean toward the positions they espouse because of their commitment to specific philosophies such as Idealism, Realism, or Pragmatism.

In this kind of classification of positions, more is taken into account than philosophy. Some of the associations are dependent upon acceptance of findings in psychology, particularly learning and child development. Nevertheless, there is a great deal of reciprocal conversation about educational philosophy and

[12]Hugh C. Black, "Confusion and Conflict in Educational Theory: an Analysis," *Peabody Journal of Education*, 30:153-160, November, 1952.

[13]Hugh C. Black, "A Four-fold Classification of Educational Theories," *Educational Theory*, 16:289, July, 1966.

educational theory even to the extent of using the two terms as synonyms.

We should not leave this discussion of philosophy and theory in education without noting the existence of two points of view about the role of the philosopher in theoretical work in education. There has been a recent thrust toward the use of language analysis as the primary tool for educational theorizing. Advocates of this technique claim that the main function of the philosopher is to clarify the language used to talk about problems. Central to this position is the gaining of skill in correct use of language and the building of more adequate logic. Opposed to the extreme posture of the linguistic analysts are the advocates of more substantive philosophy who make use of metaphysics, epistemology, and ethics in arriving at prescriptive propositions about education. In my judgment, we should not leave this as an either-or option. Educational theorizing will demand the skills of both the substantive and the analytic philosopher.[14] Too many decisions in education rest upon value orientation.

Other Approaches to Educational Theory

The problem for educational theory, like that posed for any theory, is to explain all dimensions of education and the interrelationships among its constructs and propositions. To explain all aspects of education, or even schooling as a more limited sphere of education, by prescriptive theory alone is inadequate in modern times. Descriptive theory development is also needed. Many aspects of curriculum, instruction, administration, and other components of education can be subjected to the rigors of scientific theory-building procedures. The need for educational theory is so great and the field is so broad and complicated that there is plenty of room for all who may wish to work at it regardless of the kind of theory they may wish to develop.

An appeal for such needed development in educational theory was well voiced by Broudy when he called for unifying principles to be used in the resolution of conflict associated with innovations in

---

[14]Support for this posture is given by Broudy and Mays respectively in: Harry S. Broudy, "The Philosophical Foundations of Educational Objectives," *Educational Theory*, 20:3-21, Winter, 1970, and Wolfe Mays, "Linguistic Analysis and the Philosophy of Education," *Educational Theory*, 20:269-283, Summer, 1970.

school practices. For Broudy, a unified theory of education would take into account the following factors:

   a. The present and projected kinds of knowledge and personality traits required for citizenship, vocation, and self-development.

   b. A unified theory of education must be clear about the uses of schooling.

   c. A unified theory must be judicious about the latest developments in learning theory and teaching technology.

   d. A unified theory has to provide for general and special education, for differences in ability and bent.[15]

For Broudy, a unified theory of education would rationally organize cultural objectives, life outcomes, teacher and other specialist training, and facilities and resources necessary to make the enterprise go.

A much different approach to educational theory was taken by Brauner.[16] Brauner analyzed six major traditions that have influenced American educational thought throughout the nation's history. The traditions and characteristics associated with them are presented in Figure 3. In the figure, it can be noted that method, view of the child, and a controlling theme are regarded by Brauner as the principal theoretical characteristics associated with the six traditions listed.

In addressing himself to the issue of education as a subject of analytical study, Brauner was critical of the present state of affairs. He said: "With but rare exceptions, the bulk of what is written about education fails in substance, form, and vocabulary. It fails as scholarship, as interpretation, as communication, and as guidance for instruction."[17] If Brauner's assessment is correct, educational theory rests on an unstable base. Yet educational theory is no less needed for that reason.

A growing theme in educational theorizing is the conception of education as a discipline. In the accompanying dialogue, the subject of education as a field of study, and/or as a field susceptible to theorizing, is germane. Two definitive works will be cited as examples.

---

[15]Harry S. Broudy, "Needed: A Unifying Theory of Education," *Curriculum Change: Direction and Process* (Washington: Association for Supervision and Curriculum Development, NEA, 1960), p. 24.

[16]Charles Brauner, *American Educational Theory* (Englewood Cliffs, N.J.: Prentice-Hall, Inc., 1964).

[17]*Ibid.*, p. 302.

The Tradition	Method	View of Child	Controlling Theme
Monitorial Method	Drill and Memorization	Trainable beast	Obedience
Object-Teaching	Handling Things	Flower to be cultivated	Discovery
Herbartianism	Five Steps	Social Embryo to be molded	Will power
Child Study	Self-Expression	Potential Artist	Sensitivity
Experimentalism	Problem-Solving by Scientific Method	Responsible Rebel	Involvement
Current Academic Emphasis	New Technology	Greatest Natural Resource	Mastery

Figure 3. *Six major traditions in American Education.* Adapted by permission from Charles J. Brauner, *American Education Theory* (Englewood Cliffs, N.J.: Prentice-Hall, Inc., 1964), p. 279.

A series of papers and responses to them was given at a symposium at John Hopkins University in May, 1961.[18] They were addressed to the question of whether education should be regarded as a discipline. Scholars representing various disciplines gave the papers and made comments upon the papers. Frequently, when an original paper posed education as a discipline, the comment took the opposite side. The arguments were conditioned by the ways individuals defined disciplines and related concepts. For example, a proponent of education as a discipline was opposed by a proponent of education as a profession. A discipline adds to its own knowledge; a profession is characterized by the services it renders. Education is the application of many disciplines; a discipline develops its own way of study and behaving. Obviously, the symposium was much more successful in identifying the issues involved than resolving them.

---

[18]John Walton and James L. Kuethe (eds.), *The Discipline of Education* (Madison, Wis.: The University of Wisconsin Press, 1963).

In the volume edited by Walton and Keuthe, a number of individuals with biases in their own fields of study debated and analyzed the disciplinary status of education. In yet another volume, a single author spelled out a detailed rationale for education as a discipline.[19] In the latter, Belth revived many of the arguments about why education should or should not be a discipline. He rejected the notion that education is solely the application of other disciplines, holding instead that education is a field of study (a discipline) in its own right. Education as a set of "know how to do" technical skills was rejected in deference to education conceived as the development of powers of explanation. Belth stated:

> The study of education is the study of the way in which models for inquiry are constructed, used, altered, and reconstructed. It is, further, a study of the types of models available to us at any given moment, and the conditions which make the model either employable or in need of rebuilding.[20]

The following list of what the study of education would include helps visualize Belth's point of view:

1. A history of the theories and models of education. Their development and their careers.
2. Principles and procedures for analysis of educational models.
3. The exploration of the functions of the prevailing models for the tool skills of reading and writing.
4. The study of prevailing models, revealing the modes of thinking in social, psychological, economic, and political facets of our developed culture which have given that culture its characteristic patterns of operation. An intensive study of the relationship between ways of thinking and the developed culture patterns would set forth the determining force of thought and the characteristics of the elements which enter into the act of thinking.
5. Detailed study into the variety of models by means of which a particular subject discipline is undertaken or performed (a history and analysis of the models of a discipline, or of several disciplines). In this one area especially, the theoretically grounded teacher of social studies, for example, is able, if competent in analysis, to analyze the level of education which a child has reached.
6. A period which is like the widely prevailing student teaching practice, but which is a research program and an analytical seminar in

---

[19]Marc Belth, *Education as a Discipline* (Boston: Allyn and Bacon, Inc., 1965).
[20]*Ibid.*, p. 103.

which there is opportunity for diagnosis of the efforts of the prospective teacher examining his own educational experiments in his classes.[21]

Although one may argue with the details of Belth's position, he nonetheless stimulates thought in regard to the disciplinary status of education.

It is not the purpose of this book to pursue the argument of whether education is a discipline or not. The belief that education is an organized field of study about which theories may be built, however, is another matter. There is an increasing demand for rigorous research and theory building in education. Pioneer steps in this direction were taken by individuals such as G. Stanley Hall and Edward L. Thorndike, who employed the techniques of science in solving educational problems. Most of what is done in schools, however, either is done on a trial-and-error basis or because successful practice has made it respectable. What is now needed is for clear-headed thinkers to stretch for more rational explanations of what education does and should do. Individuals who are convinced that the only worthwhile activities for students of professional education are intensive study of the organized disciplines and extensive practical experience in schools tend to lead education away from badly needed systematic self-study. It really does not matter much whether education is called a discipline, a profession, or something else. Irrespective of label, evidence mounts that education is sufficiently mature to become an organized field of study.

A third kind of evidence for the advance of thinking about educational theory is reflected in the writing and research on the use of models in educational theorizing. The most extensive work over an extended period of time in this area was done by George and Elizabeth Maccia. The final report of their project brings together the essence of many previous reports.[22] Educational theory models were reproduced from models from such areas as set theory, information theory, graph theory, and general systems theory. Ways of deducing educational research hypotheses were described by use of models and symbols borrowed from theoretical formulations external to education.

---

[21]*Ibid.*, p. 304.

[22]Elizabeth Steiner Maccia and George S. Maccia, *Development of Educational Theory Derived from Three Educational Theory Models* (Columbus, Ohio: The Ohio State University Research Foundation, 1966).

In educational theory, attention is being increasingly paid to rules for theory building as prescribed by both philosophers and behavioral scientists. These are real signs of mature development in a field of inquiry. But for sophisticated theory development in education to be realized, more has to happen. One mark of a sophisticated theory in a complex field such as education is for the theory to be undergirded by sub-theories of its components. Thus, we may say that the development of theories of administration, instruction, and curriculum would contribute to more sophisticated developments in educational theory since they are among the legitimate components of the educational enterprise. In the remainder of this chapter, we will discuss some of the theory building efforts in administration and instruction as sub-theories of educational theory even though it will not be possible to show one-to-one relationships between the developments in the sub-theories and developments in parent educational theories. We are a long way from that stage.

THEORY IN SCHOOL ADMINISTRATION

One special interest group in education, professors of school administration, has been giving serious attention to the problem of theorizing. What they have actually been doing is building a sub-theory of educational theory, namely the theory of administration. Much of their effort was sponsored by the University Council for Educational Administration, the National Conference for Professors of Educational Administration, and the Cooperative Program in Educational Administration. Individuals working on these projects have been concerned primarily with the improvement of the administration of the nation's schools and the teaching of school administration in colleges and universities, but they have used theory development as their route to improvement.

A characteristic feature of these attempts has been the insistence that education utilize the theoretical contributions of disciplines related to education, particularly those of the social sciences, for purposes of theory building in administration. Theorists in school administration have been following the same kinds of rules for theoretical work that were indicated in Chapter 2. Their efforts, for the most part, are of quite recent vintage. An early written expression of their organized effort was the signal monograph by Coladarci and Getzels in 1955.[23] A later one is the book by Halpin in 1966.[24] It is not necessary for us to review the details of these efforts here. We make note, however, of some of the uses made of fundamental theorizing procedures.

For one, the theorists in administration have employed the meanings of theory and theorizing in the accepted traditions of the other behavioral sciences. Most writers on administrative theory make use of Feigl's definition of theory, or they create a derivative from it. For example, Coladarci and Getzels recognized the predictive functions of theory when they pointed out that:

> The term "theory" is often used to mean general principles which seem to predict or account for events with an accuracy so much better than chance that we may say that the principles are "true".[25]

In discussing the construction of theories, Halpin identified the basic elements of a theory as follows:

> Theories cannot be produced on demand: they evolve, and they evolve in many shapes and in many different degrees of precision. The building blocks of which they are composed — the constructs, the postulates, the assumptions — may be molar or molecular.[26]

Griffiths listed the following steps in theory development:

1. A *description* of administrative behaviors in one situation.
2. A *definition* of certain basic concepts.
3. A more *general statement* which is descriptive of average behavior in a limited number of situations.
4. A statement of one or more *hypotheses.*
5. An *evaluation* and *reconstruction* of the hypotheses in accordance with later observations.
6. The statement of principles.[27]

---

[23]Arthur P. Coladarci and Jacob Getzels, *The Use of Theory in Educational Administration* (Stanford: School of Education, 1955).

[24]Andrew W. Halpin, *Theory and Research in Administration* (New York: The Macmillan Company, 1966).

[25]*Op. cit.*, p. 4.

[26]Andrew W. Halpin, "The Development of Theory in Educational Administration," *Administrative Theory in Education*, edited by Andrew W. Halpin (Chicago: Midwest Administration Center, University of Chicago, 1958), p. 5.

[27]Roald F. Campbell and Russell T. Gregg (eds.), *Administrative Behavior in Education* (New York: Harper and Row, 1957), pp. 363-364.

In a later writing, Griffiths presented the paradigm for theory development shown in Figure 4.

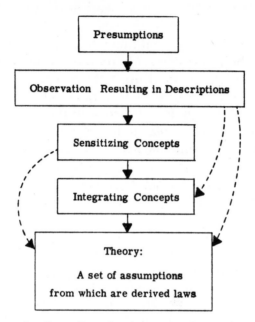

Figure 4. *Paradigm for theory development.* Adapted by permission from Daniel E. Griffiths," The Nature and Meaning of Theory," *Behavioral Science and Educational Administration,* Sixth-third Yearbook of the National Society for the Study of Education (Chicago: The University of Chicago Press, 1964), p. 104.

The foregoing illustrates the care and precision with which theorists in administration have been adhering to the kinds of rules for theorizing utilized in the behavioral sciences. The status of theory in administration is incomplete but promising. Much work has been done, but as one would expect, efforts on occasion have been at cross purposes with one another, oversimplified, or not sufficiently and carefully defined. Halpin described this condition well:

> In our efforts to develop theory in educational administration, we have been impeded by three substantive problems: (1) We have not

been clear about the meaning of theory. (2) We have tended to be preoccupied with taxonomies and have confused these with theories. (3) We have not been sure of the precise domain of the theory we are seeking to devise.[28]

Despite these negative comments, Halpin demonstrated confidence that progress would continue to be made in theory development, and he included an elaborate paradigm for research on administrator behavior.

During recent years, there has been a change in theoretical work in administration from the directions previously described. Attention has shifted to management, organizational theory, and systems development. In this sense, less attention is being paid to metatheory as a base for developing theory in administration than to theories developed from analysis of operational settings. Theoretical models are being developed that may apply to the solution of administrative problems with respect to organization and functions in various environments. These are theory-building practices but in the language of organization functions, systems analysis, role delineation, and so forth.

It also can be said that administrators are very practical people, and there is some indication that conflicts arose between the theoreticians and the practitioners in educational administration. That a gap was generated between knowledge development and knowledge utilization in administration was evidenced, for example, by the publication edited by Eidell and Kitchel.[29] In spite of some rough waters, those who have toiled so arduously at theory-building efforts in educational administration have made very real and substantial contributions to the development of administrative theory as a sub-theory of educational theory. Hopefully, their theoretical and research efforts will continue because they have truly been leaders in this activity.

INSTRUCTIONAL THEORY

A more recent development in the area of sub-theories to educational theory is the rapid growth of thinking and research pertaining to instruction. Articles on pedagogy and reports of

[28]*Theory and Research in Administration*, *op. cit.*, p. 6.
[29]Terry L. Eidell and Joanne M. Kitchel (eds.), *Knowledge, Production and Utilization* (Eugene, Ore.: The Center for the Advanced Study of Educational Administration, 1968).

research on teaching have been with us for a long time, but few, until recently, claimed to lead toward theories of instruction.

Jerome S. Bruner's book *The Process of Education*, touched off a great deal of dialogue about fundamental educational operations and conditions. The nature of instructional processes became a part of that dialogue. Then, in 1963, Bruner addressed the national conference of the Association for Supervision and Curriculum Development on the subject of theory of instruction. An adaptation of this address was published in the official journal of the association. In that article, Bruner proposed four aspects of a theory of instruction:

1. First, a theory of instruction should concern itself with the factors that predispose a child to learn effectively.
2. It should concern itself with optimal structuring of knowledge.
3. A third aspect of a theory of instruction deals with the optimal sequence that is required for learning.
4. Finally, a fourth aspect of a theory of instruction should concern itself with the nature and pacing of rewards and punishments and the successes and failures.[30]

Whether Bruner was causal or not, a flurry of activity under the general category of theories of instruction followed his presentation. Most of the activity was an inherent part of the ongoing program of the Association for Supervision and Curriculum Development. A sample of such activity merits attention here. Macdonald argued for a clarification of terms associated with instruction. As a beginning point, he suggested that a valid distinction be made among curriculum, instruction, and teaching. Having singled out instruction as an unique concept among the three terms, he then discussed as needs in research and theoretical work adequate models of instruction, empirical analysis and theory sifting from other areas, and the identification and description of criterion variables.[31]

Toward the end of 1963 and the beginning of 1964, the Association for Supervision and Curriculum Development sponsored its ninth Curriculum Research Institute. Papers from that institute were published in a pamphlet entitled *Theories of*

---

[30]Jerome S. Bruner, "A Theory of Instruction," *Educational Leadership,* 20:523-532, May, 1963.
[31]James B. Macdonald, "The Nature of Instruction: Needed Theory and Research," *Educational Leadership*, 21:5-7, October, 1963.

Instruction.[32] It is not necessary for us to review all of the elements of this publication. Most of the papers were written from the particular research bias of the authors. Individual research programs were related to theory of instruction in all cases. A major point to note here is the emphasis on carefully controlled research as a basis for reaching generalizations about teaching, or instruction, whichever term is used. These papers are an excellent illustration of the kinds of steps that need to be taken to build different theories in a given field, in this case, instruction.

A similar publication followed in 1966. This publication was an outgrowth of a joint seminar on teaching sponsored by the Association for Supervision and Curriculum Development and the Center for the Study of Instruction of the National Education Association. Here again, the emphasis was upon research in the classroom, and the authors of the included papers assumed diversified postures toward the character of research done.[33]

Also in 1966 Bruner published *Toward a Theory of Instruction.*[34] In it, Bruner expanded his previously announced, or inferred, theory of instruction. His point of departure was the same four major features of a theory of instruction previously mentioned. The foregoing publications are very illustrative of initial efforts of individuals to define and to theorize about instruction.

The position paper of the Commission on Instructional Theory of the Association for Supervision and Curriculum Development might well provide a launching platform for even more intensified effort in the development of theories of instruction.[35] The position paper was a composite of the thoughts and ideas of the various commission members. The commission, conceiving instructional theory to be a very complex phenomenon, concluded that sub-theories should be built as supports for it. This position is very much in line with the one assumed in Chapter 2, namely, that complex theories are characterized by supporting sub-theories. After debating the pros and cons of philosophical

---

[32]James B. Macdonald and Robert R. Leeper (eds.), *Theories of Instruction* (Washington: Association for Supervision and Curriculum Development, NEA, 1965).

[33]*The Way Teaching Is* (Washington: Association for Supervision and Curriculum Development and the Center for the Study of Instruction, NEA, 1966).

[34]Jerome S. Bruner, *Toward a Theory of Instruction* (Cambridge: Harvard University Press, 1966).

[35]Ira J. Gordon (ed.), *Criteria for Theories of Instruction* (Washington, D.C.: Association for Supervision and Curriculum Development, NEA, 1968).

and scientific theory, the commission took the position that it would concern itself primarily with scientific theory. The commission defined theory as follows:

> In this document the term is used in the sense in which it is used in the natural sciences to represent a set of interrelated generalizations, derived from data, which permit some degree of prediction or control over the phenomena to which they pertain. Thus a *theory of instruction* would be represented by a set of statements, based on sound replicable research, which would permit one to predict how particular changes in the educational environment would affect pupil learning.[36]

From this definition, it may be noted that research and the development of instructional theory need to be tied together. In this way theorists are encouraged to develop theories inductively from generalizations based on experimental data.

The position paper included a series of criteria which may apply to the analysis of any scientific theory, but in this case, they are focused upon the development of instructional theory. The criteria were:

1. A statement of an instructional theory should include a set of postulates and definitions of terms involved in these postulates.
2. The statement of an instructional theory or sub-theory should make explicit the boundaries of its concern and the limitations under which it is proposed.
3. A theoretical construction must have internal consistency — a logical set of interrelationships.
4. An instructional theory should be congruent with empirical data.
5. An instructional theory must be capable of generating hypotheses.
6. An instructional theory must contain generalizations which go beyond the data.
7. An instructional theory must be verifiable.
8. An instructional theory must be stated in such a way that it is possible to collect data to disprove it.
9. An instructional theory must not only explain past events but also must be capable of predicting future events.
10. At the present time, instructional theories may be expected to represent qualitative synthesis.[37]

Such statements as those above are very generalized statements that could be applied to any theory. The very difficult problem for those who would develop instructional theories is to

---

[36]*Ibid.*, p. 3.
[37]*Ibid.*, pp. 16-23.

box in the set of events subsumed under the concept "instruction." For example, do teaching and instruction have the same meanings? Is curriculum subsumed under teaching or instruction? What behaviors are associated with teaching? These questions have to be answered if one is to be serious in his intent to describe or to build anything resembling a theory of instruction.

Hosford addressed himself to these problems. He began with criteria statements and function statements for instructional theory similar to those of Bruner and Gordon, but the distinctive feature of his work is that he went much further. With criteria and functions as background, Hosford developed a basic rationale followed by postulates, laws, rules, and hypotheses as theory statements.[38]

The concept *teaching* appears to be used more broadly than the concept *instruction* especially in research. Greenberg carefully analyzed the research of Bellack, Flanders, Hughes, Smith, and Taba on classroom teaching.[39] These studies will be familiar to most readers so they need not be reviewed here. It is sufficient to say that the general approach in these studies was to analyze and classify behaviors (mostly verbal) of teachers and pupils in classrooms. They have been extremely useful to the profession in helping to identify teacher behaviors that had not previously been associated with teaching particularly through the classical methods books. Broudy distinguished three types of teaching. He identified *didactics* as the imparting and reinforcing of skill and knowledge, *heuristics* as efforts to promote discoveries by pupils, and *philetics* as behaviors associated with love or a teacher's concern for the emotional well-being of the pupil.[40] An interesting paradigm for research on teaching has been developed and used in Sweden by Dahllöf, Lundgren, and others. The paradigm has three components: frame factors, teaching process, and learning outcomes. Frame factors refer to (1) factors given in the curriculum (goals and content), (2) time available for instruction, and (3) class composition according to the ability of pupils to reach

[38]Philip L. Hosford, *An Instructional Theory – A Beginning* (Englewood Cliffs, N.J.: Prentice-Hall, Inc., 1973).

[39]Selma B. Greenberg, *Selected Studies of Classroom Teaching: A Comparative Analysis* (Scranton, Pa.: Intext Textbook Company, 1970).

[40]Harry S. Broudy, "Didactics, Heuristics and Philetics," *Educational Theory*, 22:251-261, Summer, 1972.

goals. The object of this research has been to study the effects of the frame factors upon the teaching process and resulting learning outcomes.[41] The above examples are but a small sample compared with what may be found in the *Handbook of Research on Teaching* and the *Second Handbook of Research on Teaching*. The tables of contents of those volumes would make it appear as if the field is very broad indeed. Nonetheless, there seems to be little question that a great deal of leadership in the development of components of educational theory has been demonstrated by those working upon theory building in the area of instruction.

SUMMARY

In this chapter, we have examined examples of the kinds of theorizing done within the broad field of education. The purpose in so doing was to link the discussion of Chapter 2 with subsequent discussion of curriculum theory. We have examined approaches to educational theory and two sub-theory areas of educational theory — theory in administration and instructional theory.

Meaningful relationships may be established between the work of theorists and the work of practitioners, but theory and practice are not one and the same. Theory may direct practice, or it may explain the nature of practice. Conversely, data for theory may come from practice. Theories, in turn, are tested in the crucible of practice. The relationship is reciprocal.

Individuals frequently have used traits and names of philosophies of education and theories of education interchangeably. Dimensions of philosophy have much to contribute to educational theorizing both at the level of prescriptive and descriptive theory, but philosophy and theory are not coterminous domains.

An excellent example of educational theorizing at work is in the field of school administration. Administrative theory has been developed to its present stage as a sub-theory of educational theory. Theorists in administration have disciplined themselves to use basic rules for theorizing adopted from behavioral and social sciences.

---

[41]See Urban S. Dahllof, *Ability Grouping, Content Validity, and Curriculum Process Analysis* (New York: Teachers College Press, Columbia University, 1971) and Ulf. P. Lundgren, *Frame Factors and the Teaching Process* (Stockholm: Almqvist & Wiksell, 1972).

Developments in the area of instructional theory are very encouraging. A substantial effort is being made to develop instructional theory as a sub-theory to educational theory. It is significant that the domain of theories of instruction is being discriminated from other potential areas of education such as administration and curriculum. It also is significant that theory development is being related to carefully designed research.

It is true that we are still unable to associate specific educational theories with specific sub-theories in such domains as administration, instruction, and curriculum, but the demand for bringing together the theoretical work done in the sub-theories into total educational theory is increasing. Although the dimensions of educational theory are far from being clearly identified, the profession is attempting to develop more rational explanations for those it is able to identify. The impetus to sub-theory building, the use of models for directing thinking and explanation, and the thrust of theory-oriented research are evidence of healthy activity in the area of educational theory.

SUGGESTED READINGS

Bayles, Ernest E. "Present Status of Educational Theory in the United States," *School and Society*, 87:5-8, January, 1959.

Belth, Marc. *Education As A Discipline*. Boston: Allyn and Bacon, Inc., 1965.

Black, Hugh C. "A Four-fold Classification of Educational Theories,"*Educational Theory*, 16:281-291, July, 1966.

Black, Hugh C. "Confusion and Conflict in Educational Theory: An Analysis," *Peabody Journal of Education*, 30:153-160, November, 1952.

Brauner, Charles J. *American Educational Theory*. Englewood Cliffs, N.J.: Prentice-Hall, Inc., 1964.

Broudy, Harry S. "Needed: A Unifying Theory of Education," *Curriculum Change: Direction and Process*, Robert E. Leeper, editor. Washington: Association for Supervision and Curriculum Development, NEA, 1966, pp. 15-26.

Broudy, Harry S. "The Philosophical Foundations of Educational Objectives," *Educational Theory*, 20:3-21, Winter, 1970.

Broudy, Harry S. *The Real World of the Public Schools*, New York: Harcourt Brace Jovanovich, Inc., 1972.

Bruner, Jerome S. "Needed: A Theory of Instruction," *Educational Leadership*, 20:523-532, May, 1963.

Bruner, Jerome S. *The Process of Education*. Cambridge, Mass.: Harvard University Press, 1960.

Bruner, Jerome S. *Toward A Theory of Instruction.* Cambridge, Mass.: Harvard University Press, 1966.

Burnett, Joe R. "Observations on the Logical Implications of Philosophic Theory for Educational Theory and Practice," *Educational Theory,* 11:65-70, April, 1961.

Clements, Millard. "Theory and Education," *Educational Theory.* 12:124-128, April, 1962.

Coladarci, Arthur P. and Jacob W. Getzels. *The Use of Theory in Educational Administration.* Stanford: School of Education, Stanford University, Monograph No. 5, 1955.

Dahllöf, Urban S. *Ability Grouping, Content Validity, and Curriculum Process Analysis.* New York: Teachers College Press, Teachers College, Columbia University, 1971.

Gage, N. L. (ed.). *Handbook of Research on Teaching.* Chicago: Rand McNally and Company, 1963.

Gordon, Ira J. (ed.). *Criteria for Theories of Instruction.* Washington, D.C.: Association for Supervision and Curriculum Development, NEA, 1968.

Gowin, D.B. "Can Educational Theory Guide Practice?" *Educational Theory,* 13:6-12, January, 1963.

Greenberg, Selma. *Selected Studies of Classroom Teaching: A Comparative Analysis.* Scranton, Pa.: International Textbook Company, 1970.

Griffiths, Daniel E. *Administrative Theory.* New York: Appleton-Century-Crofts, Inc., 1959.

Hadden, Eugene E. *Evolving Instruction.* New York: Macmillan Company, 1970.

Halpin, Andrew W. (ed.). *Administrative Theory in Education.* Chicago: Midwest Administration Center, University of Chicago, 1958.

Halpin, Andrew W. *Theory and Research in Administration.* New York: The Macmillan Company, 1966.

Hosford, Philip H. *An Instructional Theory – A Beginning.* Englewood Cliffs, N.J.: Prentice-Hall, Inc., 1973.

Levit, Martin. "The Study of Education," *Educational Theory,* 23:15-26, Winter, 1973.

Lundgren, Ulf P. *Frame Factors and the Teaching Process.* Stockholm, Sweden: Almqvist & Wiksell, 1972.

Maccia, Elizabeth Steiner and George S. Maccia. *Development of Educational Theory Derived from Three Educational Theory Models.* Columbus, Ohio: The Ohio State University Research Foundation, 1966.

Macdonald, James B. "The Nature of Instruction: Needed Theory and Research," *Educational Leadership,* 21:5-7, October, 1963.

Macdonald, James B. and Robert R. Leeper (eds.). *Theories of Instruction.* Washington: Association for Supervision and Curriculum Development, NEA, 1965.

Mason, Robert E. "Grounds of Acceptable Theory in Education," *Studies in Philosophy and Education,* 1:44-65, January, 1961.

Mays, Wolfe. "Linguistic Analysis and the Philosophy of Education," *Educational Theory,* 20:269-283, Summer, 1970.

Newsome, George L., Jr. "In What Sense is Theory a Guide to Practice in Education?" *Educational Theory*, 14:31-39, January, 1964.

O'Connor, D.J. *An Introduction to the Philosophy of Education*. London: Routledge and Kegan Paul, 1957.

Pratte, Richard. *Contemporary Theories of Education*. Scranton, Pa.: Intext Educational Publishers, 1971.

Rosenshine, Barak. "Evaluation of Instruction," *Review of Educational Research*, 40:279-300, April, 1970.

School and Society. 87:1-20, January, 1959.

Sizer, Theodore. "Commentary: Three Major Frustrations: Ruminations of a Retiring Dean." *National Elementary Principal*, 52:74-77, January, 1973.

Smith, B. Othanel and Robert H. Ennis (eds.). *Language and Concepts in Education*. Chicago: Rand McNally and Company, 1961.

Travers, Robert M.W. *An Introduction to Educational Research*. 3rd ed. New York: The Macmilllan Company, 1969.

Wagener, James W. "Toward a Heuristic Theory of Instruction: Notes on the Thought of Michael Polanyi," *Educational Theory*, 20:46-53, Winter, 1970.

Walton, John and James L. Kuethe (eds.). *The Discipline of Education*. Madison, Wis.: The University of Wisconsin Press, 1963.

The Way Teaching Is. Washington: Association for Supervision and Curriculum Development and the Center for the Study of Instruction, NEA, 1966.

Chapter 4

CURRICULUM THEORY

In Chapter 1, we established curriculum as a sub-system of education along with such others as instruction, evaluation, and administration. As a sub-system of education, curriculum must have unique properties and functions that distinguish it from the other sub-systems. A curriculum theory, therefore, must explain in various ways the character of and the relationships among the unique properties and functions of the curriculum sub-system. The function of this chapter is to orient basic theory-building processes to the field of curriculum and then to point out some historic exemplars of theoretical postures taken on curriculum.

THEORY PROCESSES IN CURRICULUM

From our conclusions in Chapters 2 and 3, we should impose upon the would-be curriculum theorist two kinds of guide or principle. One has to do with definition and theory content, the other with the types of activity permissible or mandatory.

Definitions and Theory Content

Initially, we stated that a theory is a set of statements. It must be in the form of a physical record that may be used as a means of communication among people and as a directive force in furthering theoretical and practical work efforts. Individual statements within a theory must be related in such a way as to produce greater meaning to the individual parts and to foster interrelation among the parts, thereby extending meaning to the whole set of events giving rise to the theory. This demand for relatedness is present in all serious writing about theory. Most series of events in curriculum are so variable that explanations for them may need to assume the form of definitions and various kinds of propositions. For a theory to explain these variant events systematically, the theory builder needs to relate them.

Theory may be defined as a set of related statements that are arranged so as to give functional meaning to a series of events. The set of related statements may take the form of descriptive or functional definitions, operational constructs, assumptions, postulates, hypotheses, generalizations, laws, or theorems. The precise contents are dictated by the scope of the series of events, the amount of empirical knowledge available, and the degree of sophistication of theory and research surrounding the series of events.

Now let us apply these basic ideas about theoretical work to curriculum theory. The first task is to define curriculum theory. If a theory is a set of related statements that are arranged so as to give functional meaning to a set or a series of events, *a curriculum theory is a set of related statements that gives meaning to a school's curriculum by pointing up the relationships among its elements and by directing its development, its use, and its evaluation.* The subject matter of curriculum theory may be the events associated with decisions about a curriculum, the use of a curriculum, the development of a curriculum, curriculum design, curriculum evaluation, and so forth.

Such events are only part of the task of identifying curriculum theory ingredients. Within each of any identified series of events, there are technical terms that define the subject matter of the theoretical field. These have to be defined, or the boundaries of the theorist's work cannot be determined. Definitions also serve a functional purpose when they can be translated into operational constructs in research.

When a theorist identifies pertinent technical concepts, he is forced to open up all aspects of the field of curriculum that need to be explained by a full-blown curriculum theory. When the theorist turns to definition of concepts, it immediately becomes apparent to him that the key concept demanding clear definition is curriculum. Three key ways of using the word *curriculum* emerge from the literature. One use of the word *curriculum* is as a substantive phenomenon. In the frame of this usage, one talks about *a curriculum*. In most cases a curriculum is a plan of some kind. It may be a plan consisting of proposed learning opportunities for school pupils. A curriculum may be thought of as a set of intended outcomes. For others, a curriculum may be an elaborate document including objectives, activities, instructional materials, and time schedules. Some conceive a curriculum as a written document; others view it as a set of verbal agreements. One authority may propose that a curriculum be made for a school or a school district. Another may propose that one be made for a state's schools. A third may propose that a curriculum should be national in scope. Regardless of meanings associated, a theorist must talk about *a curriculum*.

A second use of the word *curriculum* is a synonym for a *curriculum system*. A curriculum system is that part of the organized framework of a school or a school system within which all curriculum decisions are made. A curriculum system consists of the personnel organization and the organized procedures needed to produce a curriculum, to implement it, to appraise it, and to modify it in light of experience. The principal output of a curriculum system is a curriculum; the function of the system is to keep the curriculum dynamic.

A third use of the word *curriculum* is a synonym for an area of professional study. This mode is to speak of *curriculum as a total field of study*. This is the usage employed by nearly all professional schools of education.

A very important and substantive part of the content of any theory is the accumulation of statements describing relationships among the ingredients of the theory. To these need to be added the structural relationships between the theory being developed and its sub-theories. If we employ the three uses of curriculum as a framework, relationships among the ingredients of curriculum theory may be more readily identified. Within the concept of *a curriculum*, there are many key relationships to be described. The primary ones have to do with such matters as the relationships between goals and culture content, between school organization and scope and sequence, or between culture content and overall design. Secondary, or peripheral, relationships have to do with influences that impinge on curriculum decisions but which are not a part of a curriculum. Statements of these relationships need to explain why primary decisions are made. For example, goals are selected according to a conceived role of the school in society. Much of grade placement of subject matter depends upon predictions about the school population.

The concept of *a curriculum system* implies a governing cluster of relationships. Most of them have to do with the human engineering required in the process of curriculum development and curriculum usage. The fundamental tasks of a curriculum system set the framework for needed relationship ties. The tasks inherent in a curriculum system, briefly mentioned here and detailed in later chapters are: (1) the choice of arena for curriculum decision-making, (2) the selection and involvement of persons in curriculum planning, (3) organization for and techniques used in curriculum planning, (4) actual writing of a curriculum, (5) implementing the curriculum, (6) evaluating the curriculum, and (7) providing for feedback and modification of the curriculum. When statements of relationship among these elements are articulated, the phenomena of curriculum development, curriculum use, and curriculum evaluation will have been described. The primary concern here is one of explaining the structure and functions of a curriculum system.

The purpose of *curriculum as a field of study* is to advance knowledge about curriculums and curriculum systems. Whatever is included in the field of study must be defended on the basis of that purpose. It is conventional for students of curriculum to study social and psychological foundations of education. Advanced students study research design and procedures in depth. They study and analyze our past experiences in curriculum affairs. Establishing relationships among such studies and the basic ideas of curriculum design and engineering gives added theoretical strength to curriculum as a field of study.

To the foregoing relationship statements, others need to be added to fill out the picture of theory content in curriculum. These constitute the statements needed to show relationships between curriculum theory and the remaining sub-theories of educational theory. Figure 1 in Chapter 1 reveals some of these to be instructional theory, evaluation theory, administrative theory, and counseling theory. Relationship ties among some of these are stronger than among others. Irrespective of strength, relationships need to be described in order to clarify the unique role of curriculum theory as a sub-theory of educational theory.

Curriculum Theory-Building Activities

The curriculum theorist is subject to the same rules of behavior as any theorist in the behavioral sciences; consequently, he is obligated to engage in the most commonly accepted work practices of all. They are: (1) establishment of descriptive and prescriptive definitions for technical terms, (2) classification of existing and new knowledge, (3) inferential and predictive research, (4) sub-theory development, and development and use of models.

We have labored sufficiently over the need for establishing and consistently using definitions of technical terms. Generally, educational writers and theorists have been unwilling or unable to define their technical terms with care and to use them consistently once having defined them. It is absolutely essential for the theorist to identify and define the key terms of his field. For instance, such concepts as curriculum, subject matter, design, implementation, and evaluation are a few that would have to be carefully structured. These concepts permeate curriculum considerations.

The act of classifying knowledge is another theory function. Although a classification system is not synonymous with a theory, the former is essential to the latter. Without order and relationship, meaning for a series of events is elusive or non-existent.

Although some classification of curriculum knowledge has taken place in subordinate aspects of curriculum, a systematic classification is still lacking. This condition is strange because classification is a theory-building activity that is very possible in the field of curriculum. Limited attempts have been made by those who have raised questions that curriculum theory should answer, such as those about what content, what organization, what teaching, for what pupils, for what purposes. Progress beyond that has been inhibited by the lack of acceptance of a conceptual framework for curriculum classification. Probably, the lack of advance in classification is primarily attributable to great variation in use of technical terms. The effect is to produce a reluctance to postulate a classification scheme and expose it to the light of research and experience.

Inference and prediction are of the highest order in the work of the theorizer. It is possible for one to arrive at definitions, descriptions, and classification schemes initially by analytical procedures or by simple descriptive research, but it is not possible for one to go beyond those levels without the kinds of research that will allow one to infer or predict from the results. The kinds of research from which inference and prediction may be made are assigned various names in research literature. We will note here only the two most relevant research techniques. First, it should be stated that the act of inferring is a logical process. An inference is a proposition or generalization derived from evidence by reasoning. The research design does not provide the inference.

With one type of problem, a researcher is concerned with the examination of differences between, or among, samples taken from a known population. Measures for a criterion, or dependent, variable are taken from all samples, and various treatments are assigned to individual sample groups so as to manipulate independent variable effects. The researcher, in these cases, usually seeks causal relationships between the criterion variable and the independent variables. It is common for analysis of variance designs and techniques to be used in these cases to examine the relationships. The researcher reaches a conclusion from observation of the results of his data treatment. Providing he is satisfied with the validity and reliability of his conclusion, the researcher can infer that his conclusion is generalizable to all samples of the population. A simple illustration in curriculum research would be a study of the effects of various kinds of inservice training administered to randomly selected groups of teachers upon their ability to participate as curriculum planners. The results, assuming proper controls and treatments, would permit the researcher to infer that the same status would hold for other similarly chosen groups and their parent population.

In a sense, prediction is a special case of inference. For predictive relationships, research is designed so that one can estimate the unknown from the known. However, it is first necessary to establish the relationship between the known and the unknown characteristics or behaviors. A commonly-used research technique for this kind of problem is correlation and regression analysis. A study is made of the correlation between two or more sets of behaviors or characteristics that are assumed to be related. The purpose of such a study is to establish the strength of the relationship so that thereafter one can predict one of the sets of behaviors or characteristics (the unknown) from the other (the known). The well-known correlation between measures of intelligence and measures of school achievement was observed, and we feel confident, within established limits, that we can predict school achievement once intelligence has been measured satisfactorily. In curriculum, many needs for research of this kind exist. A curriculum itself is an expression of prediction. Curriculum planners predict that teachers will use a curriculum as a point of departure for their teaching; otherwise there would be little point in doing all that work. Curriculum planners may predict that certain learning outcomes will occur. Rarely have these predictions been tested out in research, but they must be to develop generalizations about the phenomena for purposes of building curriculum theory.

A mature theory is undergirded by sub-theories. If they seek mature curriculum theories, curriculum theorists must work at identifying and building the sub-theories of curriculum. What the sub-theories are may be dependent upon the concepts and procedures the theorist wishes to associate with the field of curriculum. Possibilities for sub-theories to curriculum theory are curriculum design, procedures for curriculum planning and implementation, and curriculum evaluation. Accounting for these functions theoretically is the domain of sub-theory building in curriculum, and we will address ourselves to these areas in later chapters.

Model building is another activity for the curriculum theorist, and the theorist may use models in a variety of ways. Models may be used to illustrate a person's posture on the design of a curriculum. Models are useful in depicting procedures for curriculum planning and implementation. Curriculum evaluation schema may be represented by models. Models may be created to show relationships among curriculum design, the curriculum engineering processes, and evaluation processes. The latter would be a basic model of a curriculum theory. It makes little difference whether models are "borrowed" as paradigms from other areas of knowledge or whether they are developed indigenously within the framework of curriculum constructs originally.

Progress in curriculum theory has been slow and meager, and too few curriculum specialists have responded to the need for thoughtful theoretical work. Like many other functions in education, the curriculum function has responded more to the external pressures from an expanding culture than to internal examination, systematic research, and explanation. In responding to the set of external forces, curriculum workers have been busy, and they have worked diligently, and at all times, creatively. We shall now turn to some of those efforts.

EXEMPLARS IN CURRICULUM THINKING

From the history of curriculum thought one can glean persistent ideas that may be said to have theoretical bases, and there is evidence that a body of concern by curriculum scholars is emerging toward a field of curriculum theory. To a very great extent, the bases for most of the postures represented here are rooted in the educational ethos of the period of our history in which they developed; yet, there has evolved a series of persistent problems that may be said to belong to curriculum.

The history of curriculum thought has been reviewed from time to time. Two examples will be cited here. Seguel reviewed the formative years of the curriculum field which she stipulated to be between 1890 and 1940.[1] Seguel chose to illustrate periodic developments in curriculum by describing the work of representative scholars. Charles and Frank McMurry were selected as representatives of the Herbartian movement. John Dewey was included because of his pervasive influence upon the curriculum thinking of all others. Franklin Bobbitt and Werrett W. Charters were chosen to represent the movement in curriculum known as activity analysis. Harold Rugg represented a group attempting to synthesize ideas about curriculum up to that point in time. And Hollis Caswell was selected to represent the new specialist in curriculum making. Phillips analyzed meanings

---

[1]Mary Louise Seguel, *The Curriculum Field: Its Formative Years* (New York: Teachers College Press, Columbia University, 1966).

associated with the concept "curriculum" from its early use to the year 1962.[2] He divided his analysis into three chronological periods, namely, (1) the Pre-Progressive Period from 1890 to 1918, (2) the Progressive Period from 1918 to 1955, and (3) the Post-Progressive Period after 1955. Phillips then identified the curriculum postures of writers within those periods. For our purposes in this writing, we will divide our attention between the periods of 1918 to 1950 and from 1950 to the present. From the viewpoint of curriculum theory, this rough division seems appropriate since 1950 marked the publication of the proceedings of a major conference on curriculum theory.

Early Curriculum Specialists

Although persons developed concern for curriculum problems as early as 1890, as pointed out by Seguel and Phillips, the first definitive work on general curriculum was published by Bobbitt in 1918.[3] Bobbitt really was the first of a long line of people who became curriculum specialists in the sense that they developed a curriculum posture and were leaders in the practical affairs of curriculum development. Bobbitt is identified as a proponent of activity analysis as a means of making curriculum decisions. He was among the first to use the methods of science to identify the activities and predispositions of adults for purposes of creating a school curriculum that would prepare children for that kind of adult life. Bobbitt's rationale is depicted in the following statement:

> The central theory is simple. Human life, however varied, consists in the performance of specific activities. Education that prepares for life is one that prepares definitely and adequately for these specific activities. However numerous and diverse they may be for any social class, they can be discovered. This requires only that one go out into the world of affairs and discover the particulars of which these affairs consist. These will show the abilities, attitudes, habits, appreciations, and forms of knowledge that men need. These will be the objectives of the curriculum. They will be numerous, definite, and particularized. The curriculum will then be that series of experiences which children and youth must have by way of attaining those objectives.[4]

---

[2]Richard C. Phillips, "A Historical Study of the Concept Curriculum" (unpublished doctor's dissertation, Northwestern University, Evanston, Illinois, 1962).

[3]Franklin Bobbitt, *The Curriculum* (Boston: Houghton Mifflin Company, 1918).

[4]*Ibid.*, p. 42.

Charters was much in agreement with Bobbitt in proposing job analysis of adult occupations as a technique for formulating bases for curriculum decisions.[5] In this respect, Charters was more concerned with vocational education. Both reached similar conclusions about curriculum content.

Two things stand out about the theoretical postures of Bobbitt and Charters. First, they were committed to the use of the techniques of science in the solution of curriculum problems. In this respect, they were influenced by the scientific movement in education led by persons such as E. L. Thorndike, Charles Judd, and their followers. Second, Bobbitt and Charters held, as a basis for their theories, the assumption that it was the function of the school to prepare the young for adult life. The way to find out about adult life was to analyze it, and the way to make a curriculum was to decide what skills, knowledge, values, and attitudes would prepare the school leavers to participate in that life. The whole approach was a vigorous way of determining curriculum content and objectives and for organizing the curriculum content in a systematic manner.

Under the leadership of the Progressives, the child-centered movement was causal in a shift in the whole character of curriculum thinking beginning early in the 1920's. Attention was shifted from the organization of subject matters aimed at preparation for adult life to the psychological behavior of the learner in the present. The important criteria for curriculum content became the interests and needs of children in school. Since the interests and needs of children emerged from their daily experience, a pre-planned curriculum without the involvement of the children in the planning became an anathema to the development of a good educational program.

The conflict between the society-centered and the child-centered groups was brought into sharp focus in the Twenty-sixth Yearbook of the National Society for the Study of Education.[6] The society's committee was composed of persons of various persuasions, and Harold Rugg was chairman. In spite of differences in theoretical orientation, the committee was able to

---

[5]Werrett W. Charters, *Curriculum Construction* (New York: The Macmillan Company, 1923).

[6]Harold Rugg, Chairman, *The Foundations and Technique of Curriculum Construction*, Twenty-sixth Yearbook of the National Society for the Study of Education, Part I and II (Bloomington, Ill.: Public School Publishing Company, 1927).

formulate a statement of working principles for curriculum making. That statement of principles came as close to being a statement of curriculum theory as anything set forth up to that time. It is interesting to note that committee members each prepared a supplementary statement to the general statement of principles in order to preserve the integrity of their own orientations. In those statements, one can find the theoretical postures of the conflicting viewpoints highlighted. It is a curious thing that efforts of this kind have not been repeated with regularity so that the likenesses and differences of curriculum positions would be kept as clear as they were illuminated by those theorists in 1927.

Following Seguel's idea, we will use Hollis Caswell as a representative of a different breed of curriculum specialist from the groups previously discussed. Caswell set virtually a performance model for leadership in curriculum development during his association with the Division of Surveys and Field Studies at Peabody College for Teachers in Nashville, Tennessee. During this period of his life, Caswell was involved as a consultant to curriculum development projects in Alabama, Florida, Virginia, and others.[7] We can see in the work of Caswell and his associates increased emphasis upon teacher involvement in curriculum decisions, organizational structures for planning groups, and such steps in procedure as defining the meaning of curriculum, determining objectives, selecting content, determining curriculum design, and measuring outcomes.

Thus, we see most of the basic theoretical curriculum issues highlighted by curriculum scholars early in the development of the field. We see the argument about basic philosophy of the school as a social institution through the curriculum postures taken by persons who were either society-centered, child-centered, or interactive in their basic outlooks. We see basic issues about curriculum design ranging from formal organization of school subjects to the experience notion. And we see issues about the selection and involvement of persons in curriculum building tasks as well as the tasks themselves. However, the more or less technical aspects of curriculum theory building really did not begin to enter the literature until the 1950's.

---

[7]Seguel, *op. cit.*, pp. 137-175.

Later Developments

About mid-twentieth century, discussions of curriculum theory *qua* theory began to appear in the literature. The first large-scale discussion of curriculum theory took place at the University of Chicago in 1947. The papers presented at that conference were published in a monograph in 1950.[8] Each author of a paper was given virtually complete freedom to treat his topic individually. inasmuch as the composite papers made no pretense at covering the field of curriculum theory comprehensively. It is significant to observe that in one of the overview sections of the report, the following three-fold task for curriculum theory was prescribed:

> (1) to identify the critical issues or points in curriculum development and their underlying generalizations; (2) to point up the relationships which exist between these critical points and their supporting structure; and (3) to suggest and to forecast the future of approaches made to resolve these critical issues.[9]

And in a concluding chapter the following challenge was issued:

> As a further effort in hastening the communications between groups of interested people and in the development of more adequate theory, someone might spend time trying to describe the nature of such theory, its tasks, its subject matter, its tests, and its uses.[10]

What has come to be called the Tyler rationale was published in 1950. The rationale revolves around four central questions:

1. What educational purposes should the school seek to attain?
2. What educational experiences can be provided that are likely to attain these purposes?
3. How can these educational experiences be effectively organized?
4. How can we determine whether these purposes are being attained?[11]

This formulation has been the one most persistently used with reference to curriculum theory since its publication. The questions raised by Tyler had been raised by other curriculum scholars

---

[8]Virgil E. Herrick and Ralph W. Tyler (eds.), *Toward Improved Curriculum Theory*, Supplementary Educational Monograph, Number 71 (Chicago: University of Chicago Press, 1950).

[9]*Ibid.*, p. 1.

[10]*Ibid.*, p. 121.

[11]Ralph W. Tyler, *Basic Principles of Curriculum and Instruction* (Chicago: University of Chicago Press, 1950), pp. 1-2.

before him, but his unique statement has been well popularized.

At least in partial response to the challenge issued in the Herrick and Tyler monograph previously cited, namely, that someone might spend time trying to describe the nature of curriculum theory, the first edition of this book (*Curriculum Theory*) appeared in 1961. It was the first single volume to present an organized statement of the status and dimensions of curriculum theory based upon conceptual structures and relationships derived from theory building efforts in closely related disciplines. The second edition (1968) was done in the same spirit.

Two papers given at the 1963 National Conference of the Association for Supervision and Curriculum Development contributed to the dialogue about curriculum theory. The conference, in part, consisted of a series of seminars one of which had curriculum theory as its topic. Two papers were given at the seminar which pointed up a major dilemma in curriculum theory, and the dilemma remains unresolved at this writing. The paper titles reveal the two sides.

One of the papers was given by Beauchamp wherein he analyzed the approach of the scientist to the tasks of theory building in curriculum.[12] In this presentation, curriculum theory was related conceptually to theory building in other domains of knowledge. The basic principles common to all, as seen by the scientist, were stressed. Careful and consistent use of technical terminology, analysis and classification of knowledge and conjecture, and the use of predictive research to increase the number of firm generalizations, or laws, were cited as principles that would give better explanation for curriculum phenomena.

The second paper has as its theme the role of philosophy in the development of scientific curriculum theory.[13] In the paper, Smith outlined three principal tasks with which philosophy can deal in aiding the curriculum theorist: (1) to formulate and justify educational purposes, (2) to select and organize knowledge, and (3) to deal with verbal traps. In identifying these three tasks, Smith

---

[12]George A. Beauchamp, "Developing a Scientific Theory in Curriculum." A paper presented at the national conference of the Association for Supervision and Curriculum Development, NEA, St. Louis, Missouri, 1963.

[13]B. Othanel Smith, "The Role of Philosophy in the Development of Scientific Curriculum Theory." A paper presented at the national Conference of the Association for Supervision and Curriculum Development, NEA, St. Louis, 1963.

noted several weaknesses in the development of curriculum theory. Too frequently, he said, curriculum theorists fail to recognize the interrelationships between educational objectives and the content of a school program. Sometimes the content itself becomes an objective, or a series of objectives. Too often, criteria for selection of content or objectives are not apparent, if they exist at all. In selecting content, a curriculum theorist must take into account the nature and structure of knowledge. He will be at great disadvantage if he fails to discriminate among factual information, values, and general principles. All of these kinds of problems are intimately related to the language used in curriculum theorizing. Progress is inhibited when basic concepts that are repeatedly used need clarification.

We note here that these two papers brought several facets of curriculum theory into sharp focus. One is that theorizing about curriculum is not solely a matter of establishing facts and relationships among empirical data. More than that, the theorist must be concerned with choices and the consequences of those choices, and at this point, the world of values confronts him. The theorist is concerned with choices at the levels of selection of purposes and content in response to those purposes. Science is of little help to him here. However, a disciplined language is a necessity whether he is calling upon the techniques of science or the wisdom of philosophy.

The use of models in theoretical work also has invaded curriculum theory efforts. A very useful contribution in this area was made by Macdonald in a paper given at a meeting of professors of curriculum.[14] In this paper, Macdonald distinguished four systems prevalent in schooling: curriculum, instruction, teaching, and learning. By use of a Venn-type diagram, he identified the interactions of the four systems. Then he analyzed the curriculum system using a general systems model characterized by the components of input, content and process, output, and feedback. At least two unique ideas emerge from Macdonald's paper. One is that we can clarify our thinking about curriculum if it is identified as a unique system of schooling. The other is that the use of the

---

[14]James B. Macdonald, "Curriculum Theory: Problems and A Prospectus." Mimeographed, a paper presented at the Professors of Curriculum meeting, Miami Beach, April, 1964.

general systems approach helps to define the kind and scope of conceptualizations needed in curriculum theory.

A slightly different schema for schooling was developed by Broudy, Smith, and Burnett. It is shown in Figure 5. In it, curriculum is depicted as part of a total system of influence directed at students. Modes of teaching are included as part of the curriculum components in the diagram, but in the accompanying text, the authors state: "Although modes of teaching are not, strictly speaking, a part of the curriculum, for practical purposes it is not useful to ignore them entirely in curriculum theory."[15] This statement would lead us to believe that Broudy, Smith, and Burnett would not significantly disagree with Macdonald's distinction between curriculum and teaching.

Beauchamp reviewed the progress made in curriculum theory between the years 1960 and 1965.[16] As a framework for discussing the research and writings about curriculum theory, he identified six components of curriculum as a field of study. These were foundational influences, subject matters, curriculum design, curriculum engineering, evaluation and research, and theory building. He noted that most progress was being made in the areas of subject matters and curriculum engineering.

Faix applied structural-functional analysis as derived from biology, sociology, and anthropology to the task of refining curriculum concepts. A curriculum function was described as what is done; a curriculum structure, as how it is done. In other words, curriculum functions describe the process by which curriculum structures are maintained or changed. A list of questions raised by a structural-functional analysis of curriculum phenomena was presented, and the titles and sub-titles of the list were termed a tentative classification of curriculum phenomena. They were: (1) general questions about curriculum phenomena, (2) questions about a curriculum system, (3) questions about units of analysis and elements, (4) questions about the structure of a curriculum system, (5) questions about the functions of a curriculum system, (6) questions about curriculum processes, and (7) general questions

---

[15]*Ibid.*, p. 79.

[16]George A. Beauchamp, "Progress in Curriculum Theory 1960-1965," Mimeographed, a paper presented at the annual conference of the American Educational Research Association, NEA, Chicago, 1965.

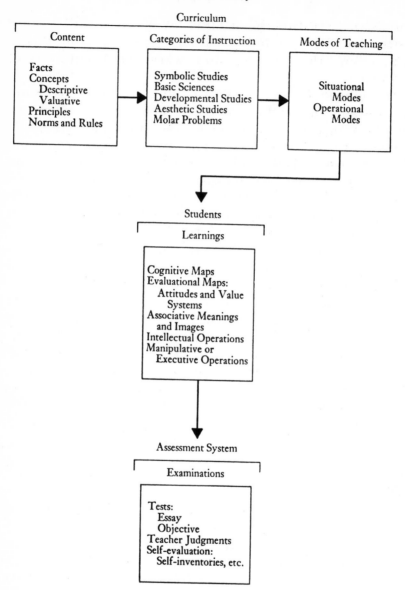

Figure 5. *A schema for schooling.* Adapted by permission from Harry S. Broudy, B. Othanel Smith, and Joe R. Burnett, *Democracy and Excellence in American Secondary Education* (Chicago: Rand McNally and Company, 1964), p. 78.

about structural-functional analysis procedures.[17] Since classification is a foundational step in scientific theory construction, this contribution warrants attention and development.

Maccia analyzed four types of curriculum theory: curriculum theory (event theory), formal curriculum theory, valuational curriculum theory, and praxiological curriculum theory.[18] Curriculum theory (event theory) was described as the sorting out and characterizing of events and relating them. In this connection, Maccia suggested that curriculum could be subsumed by a theory of instruction, thereby intimating that curriculum theory should be a sub-theory of instructional theory. Formal curriculum theory is focused on the structure of curriculum content. Valuational curriculum theory is concerned with the issue of what instructional content is the most valuable to present. And praxiological curriculum theory is speculation about appropriate curriculum means for reaching curriculum objectives. We may not agree with Maccia that so many labels are needed, or with the meanings she has assigned to curriculum, but she does help us to see more clearly that curriculum theory has several dimensions such as classification, design, values, and operations, all of which must be accounted for in a full explanation of curriculum theory.

A very interesting analysis of the use of definitions and models in curriculum theorizing was made by Johnson.[19] Whereas Maccia had implied that the definition of curriculum should emerge from the results of theory building, Johnson insisted upon a definition of curriculum as a directive force for the theory builder. He claimed that past efforts in curriculum theory have been either programmatic or analytical and that the programmatic works have been concerned with curriculum positions with primary emphasis upon curriculum development. Johnson distinguished between curriculum and the process of curriculum development. For him, a curriculum is the output of a curriculum development system, but the curriculum development system is not curriculum. We clarify

[17]Thomas L. Faix, "Structural-Functional Analysis as a Conceptual System for Curriculum Theory and Research: A theoretical Study," Mimeographed: a paper presented at the annual meeting of the American Educational Research Association, NEA, Chicago, 1966.

[18]Elizabeth Steiner Maccia, "Curriculum Theory and Policy." Mimeographed, a paper presented at the annual meeting of the American Educational Research Association, NEA, Chicago, 1965.

[19]Mauritz Johnson, Jr., "Definitions and Models in Curriculum Theory," *Educational Theory*, 17:127-140, April, 1967.

this a little more by noting that Johnson depicted curriculum as a structured series of intended learning outcomes. Curriculum so conceived relates to intentions rather than to occurrences. Under this definition, experiences that pupils have under the jurisdiction of a school become part of the domain of instruction. Like Faix, Johnson winds up his analysis with a six-point schema for curriculum:

1. A curriculum is a structured series of intended learning outcomes.
2. *Selection* is an essential aspect of curriculum formulation.
3. *Structure* is an essential characteristic of curriculum.
4. Curriculum guides instruction.
5. Curriculum evaluation involves validation of both selection and structure.
6. Curriculum is the criterion for instructional evaluation.[20]

Others before Johnson have depicted a curriculum as the output of a curriculum system and the input of an instructional system. It is necessary for a system to have both input and output geared to the feedback from evaluation in order to maintain the steady state that is characteristic of a system.

Johnson later reinforced and amplified his position that a curriculum is designed to promote and guide instructional planning which in turn guides instruction leading to learning outcomes.[21] Using a rationale very similar to that of Johnson, Posner analyzed the components of education and stated that curriculum, instruction, and learning outcomes are the components needing clarification. He claimed that, for purposes of theory and research, curriculum must be conceived to be product-oriented, prior to instruction, and descriptive.[22]

Frymier reported on a series of discussions about curriculum theory held with his colleagues at Ohio State University.[23] He took the position that curriculum consists of three basic elements: actors, artifacts, and operations. Actors, according to Frymier, are persons directly involved with curriculum. Artifacts are the

---

[20]*Ibid.*, pp. 136-139.

[21]Mauritz Johnson, Jr. "The Translation of Curriculum Into Instruction," *Educational Theory*, 1:115-131, May, 1969.

[22]George J. Posner, "Education: Its Components and Constructs." Mimeographed, a paper presented at the Annual Convention of the American Educational Research Association, Chicago, Illinois, April, 1972.

[23]Jack R. Frymier, "Around and Around the Curriculum Bush or In Quest of Curriculum Theory." A paper presented at the meeting of Professors of Curriculum, Dallas, Texas, 1967.

content of the curriculum including design problems. Operations are the processes involving the interaction of actors and artifacts. The basic unit for study in curriculum is to include three phases: (1) that which is planned, (2) that which occurs, and (3) the evaluation.

In his provocative book, *The Open Access Curriculum*, Wilson proposed that curriculum theory is most properly conceived as humanistic rather than scientific and that open access curriculum theory will be a compatible combination of knowledge theory, environmental theory, and management theory.[24]

Goodlad and Richter reported the results of their deliberations on the development of a conceptual system for dealing with problems of curriculum and instruction.[25] The study used the Tyler rationale as its primary point of departure but considerably expanded and operationalized its constructs. A conceptual system was defined as ". . . a carefully engineered framework designed to identify and reveal relationships among complex, related, interacting phenomena. . . ."[26] The authors thus conceived a conceptual system to be more general than a theory but a basis for directing theory building.

The report depicted the authors' analysis of the process of constructing what they called a rational curriculum. The process principally consisted of making use of man's funded knowledge and conventional wisdom as data sources for curriculum decisions. Utilizing these sources, curriculum decision makers would identify pertinent values to be used in deriving educational aims. Decisions about educational aims would lead to general behavioral objectives. From behavioral objectives the identification of behavioral and substantive elements follow and lead to decisions about learning opportunities and organizing centers for students. We will return to many of the details of this very well-conceived curriculum rationale as it applies to our discussions of curriculum engineering and curriculum design as sub-theories of curriculum theory.

The curriculum field continues to be explored historically.

---

[24]L. Craig Wilson, *The Open Access Curriculum* (Boston: Allyn and Bacon, Inc., 1971), p. 65.

[25]John I. Goodlad and Maurice N. Richter, Jr., "The Development of a Conceptual System for Dealing with Problems of Curriculum and Instruction," Report of an inquiry supported by The Cooperative Research Program of the Office of Education, U.S. Department of Health, Education, and Welfare, Contract No. SAE-8024, Project No. 454, 1966.

[26]*Ibid.*, p. 1.

Bellack reviewed studies of the historical development of curriculum thought and practice.[27] Kliebard analyzed the curriculum field from its beginnings.[28] He concluded that the basic problem of the curriculum field is one of self-identification, and suggested that we ". . . create a dialogue among ourselves and with our professional forebears."[29] Alpren and Baron reviewed curriculum literature in search of procedural options for developing curriculum. They identified seven: (1) adult surveys, (2) job analysis, (3) teacher committees, (4) analysis of the sources of objectives, (5) disciplinary structures, (6) behavior modification, and (7) humanistic-individualistic. It was suggested that an eighth was emerging, namely, interdisciplinary curriculum development.[30] Short examined the state of knowledge in the curriculum field. He was able to depict six categories of personnel involved in the scholarship, nineteen kinds of curriculum activity, and thirty-four types of scholarly source material produced.[31] Such historical and analytical efforts in curriculum are not specifically theory development, but they do help us see more clearly the dimensions of the total field within which the theorizing must be done.

EMERGING STATUS OF CURRICULUM THEORY

From the foregoing and other exemplars in curriculum thinking and the identified processes essential for curriculum theory building, an emerging status of curriculum theory can be explicated. It is said repeatedly in curriculum literature that a need exists for dialogue between and among curriculum theorists and practitioners about debatable issues in curriculum. The intention of this claim is that such debate would help to define a tradition of content for the curriculum field. It also is said repeatedly in

---

[27]Arno A. Bellack, "History of Curriculum Thought and Practice," *Review of Educational Research*, 39:283-292, June, 1969.

[28]Herbert M. Kliebard, "The Curriculum Field in Retrospect," *Technology and the Curriculum*, ed. Paul W.F. Witt (New York: Teachers College Press, Columbia University, 1968), pp. 69-84.

[29]*Ibid.*, p. 83.

[30]Morton Alpren and Bruce G. Baron, "Procedural Options in Developing Curriculum." Mimeographed. A paper presented at the Annual Convention of the American Educational Research Association, Chicago, Illinois, April 4, 1972.

[31]Edmund C. Short, "Curriculum Scholarship: Sources of Knowledge for the Curriculum Field," *A Search for Valid Content for Curriculum Courses*, 1970/Educational Comment (Toledo: College of Education, University of Toledo, 1970), pp. 7-19.

curriculum literature that the substance for the called-for dialogue is not known or recognized. I disagree with these laments for it seems to me that certain substantive problems and issues are before us, and most of them have been for some time. In the following paragraphs, I shall indicate what some of these substantive problems and issues are under the general categories of: (1) curriculum definition, (2) sources of curriculum decisions, (3) issues and problems of curriculum design, (4) issues and problems of curriculum engineering, and (5) theory implications.

Curriculum Definition

There is grave need for the definition of the existant range of meanings that are to be associated with the scope of events that belong to the curriculum field. The definitional behavior must answer such questions as: Is curriculum a concept unique to schooling? Does curriculum include instruction or teaching? To what extent are pupil learnings a part of curriculum? What is the total scope of curriculum as a field of study?

The above are general questions about the character of the curriculum field. There is specific need to define the range of meanings about what the ingredients of a curriculum are. This definitional process would generate the characteristics of curriculum design. Should a curriculum contain a set of behavioral or other kind of objectives? Should a curriculum contain recommended, or prescribed, content that may be used to achieve the objectives? Should a curriculum specify instructional plans and materials? Similarly, there is specific need to identify the range of meanings associated with curriculum planning, implementation, and evaluation. Some of the options in definition of curriculum design and curriculum engineering will be discussed later. The point I wish to make here is that the process of carefully and consistently defining significant curriculum areas, terms, and operational constructs is recognized in literature even though it may not be done well or by enough people.

Sources of Curriculum Decisions

When the curriculum field has been analyzed historically, clusters of sources, or foundational considerations for curriculum decisions are enumerated with considerable consistency. A number of these have been mentioned previously, but they bear repetition here. I make no claim that the cited examples are exhaustive, but the ones indicated here are before us as curriculum people, and they are sources for debate for both theoreticians and practitioners.

Early curriculum scholars advocated the adult survey and job analysis as principal bases for determining curriculum content. To some extent, certain aspects of these proposals are still with us. Advocates would say that there ought to be some relation between school life and post-school life. The concept of transfer of training is not only important for the sequential organization of subject matter in the curriculum, it is relevant to school and post-school life too. Curricula for vocational education, for example, still demand constant examination of this kind.

Man's accumulated culture is a well-recognized source but one in which there are options that have been debated heatedly, and we will profit if the debate continues. One proposal is to select curriculum content only from the recognized disciplines. Another is that there is a body of basic subject matter for schools. A third is that subject matters should be integrated. With growth in man's funded knowledge, curriculum planning is more and more becoming a process of careful selection and organization.

The student as a source is frequently placed in opposition to the culture content source. The rally cry is that the interests and needs of students must be satisfied. At least three approaches to this source of information are advocated. One is to conduct needs assessment programs to furnish data for curriculum decisions. A second is the identification and description of developmental stages of children and youth. A third is much more radical, and that is to simply have the student tell you what he wishes as his curriculum.

Culture-, or society-centered sources, and learner-centered sources are not mutually eliminating in modern thinking. Most theorists of today would insist that it must be both, but where they divide is on the point of primary emphasis. For one group, the school is primarily an agency of society in rearing of children and youth, but the children and youth are respected members of the social group who have interests and needs that must be satisfied within the culture of the school. For another group, the learner and his emerging needs must dominate decisions about school curricula, but there are bodies of culture content that are significant for learner development.

Certainly, our past experience in curriculum affairs is a source for curriculum decisions. Curricula for our schools have evolved through many stages from that of the Dame Schools of New England to those of the expanded and complex elementary and secondary schools of today. We have a history of curriculum developments in individual schools, school districts, states, and in the large national-level projects of the 1960's. This body of experience is an idea resource for those who make curriculum decisions either as to curriculum content or processes.

The values held by those concerned with determining the nature of the curriculum are an extremely dynamic source for decision making. The primary curriculum question is: What ought to be taught in the school? It is essentially a value question that must be answered by the decision makers, and the decision makers have to make use of recognized values in two ways. One is to determine what values are to be taught through the implementation of the curriculum in the school, and the other is to identify what values they are going to use for themselves as rule-governing behavior, or criteria, in making curriculum decisions. We shall discuss the significance of values in curriculum theory in greater detail in the next chapter.

Finally, we must consider social and political authority as a source for curriculum decisions. In the United States, the local board of education, acting under the authority of the state, is the policy-making body for school operations. The curriculum for a school under the jurisdiction of the board is the most important policy the board has to make. It is true that many others may participate in the development of a curriculum, but the ultimate decision that the planned curriculum is the one to be implemented through the instructional program of the schools is made by the school board. From time to time, state legislatures pass laws demanding that certain subject matters be taught in all schools in the state. State departments of education prescribe school codes that affect curriculum decisions. Parent and teacher groups have exerted tremendous influence. In recent years, teacher unions are

demanding greater voice in curriculum determination. Such
authorities are more valuable for curriculum decisions as a source,
or resource, than when they are left to act in judgment after the fact
of a curriculum that has been planned and implemented.

Curriculum Design Issues

Curriculum design has been under discussion in curriculum
literature for years. Some of the issues that have been debated are
very clear; others are less so. Nonetheless, the acceptance of a point
of view is essential in theory building, and divergent points of view
should lead to different theories.

One very clear and simply stateable issue in curriculum design
revolves around whether a curriculum should be a written
document or not. Most contemporary curriculum specialists would
advocate that curricula should be expressed in written form.
Others feel that commitment in writing is in itself restrictive upon
teachers in planning for teaching. The latter have less concern for
structure in curriculum than the former.

The sphere of the curriculum is very important conceptually.
Is a curriculum a design for a particular level of school such as the
elementary school, the middle school, or the secondary school? Is
the curriculum a design for an entire school district regardless of
how many levels of school there are? Should a curriculum include
all subjects so that a total conception of an educational plan is
expressed? Is it appropriate to talk about a mathematics
curriculum? These questions have to be answered in order to take a
posture on curriculum design.

The contents of a curriculum are debated at length. Some
would project that a curriculum should be only a set of intended
learning outcomes. The language of goals, aims, and objectives are
employed here. An important issue is whether or not the
statements should be in the form of behavioral objectives. Others
contend that a curriculum should contain more than statements of
intended outcomes whether they are stated behaviorally or not.
The content, or subject matter, to be used as means for achieving
objectives is considered by some to be a necessary ingredient of a
curriculum. Issues are present in discussions about the nature of
the content and its organization. Advocates of discipline-centered

organization are opposed by those who push for integrated subject matters. Added to these are the issues of scope, sequence, and articulation. Those who believe that a curriculum should be an expression of both what to teach and how to teach would want included matters of method, instructional materials, evaluation plans, and so forth. The posture in curriculum theory one assumes with respect to the content of a curriculum inevitably will be of great influence upon the remainder of his position.

Issues in Curriculum Engineering

The most clear-cut issue in curriculum engineering has to do with who will be involved in curriculum planning. Individuals on one side of the issue propose that teachers should be the dominant group to be involved. Their opponents would prefer that specialists in the subject or discipline areas should do the job. Related to this issue is some confusion between involvement in planning and involvement in implementation of the curriculum once it is planned. The involvement of lay citizens is both proposed and opposed.

Curriculum implementation is more of a problem than an issue. Once a curriculum is planned, its implementation is not at issue, but how it is to be implemented, including leadership in the process, becomes a problem. Our history indicates that there have been many curriculum planning efforts wasted because leadership has not been exercised over the implementation process.

Similarly, curriculum evaluation is more of a problem than an issue. Everyone agrees that a curriculum should be evaluated. The problem is how. The use of achievement measures as the sole criterion for curriculum evaluation is an indication of the need for additional alternatives.

If curricula are to be planned in local schools or school districts, the above issues and problems in curriculum engineering are symptoms of need for a deliberate system within school organization for making and executing decisions involved in curriculum planning, implementation, and evaluation. However, the details of such systems cannot be conceptualized unless the arena (the school, the district, the state, or other) has been identified. Some will claim that the "real" theoretical issues of curriculum are those associated with curriculum design and that the practical affairs of curriculum in schools and school systems are praxiological and therefore not theoretical. I choose to differ with this notion. I believe that curriculum theory is just as concerned with explanation of curriculum engineering as it is with explanation of curriculum design. Hence, we will return to more elaborate discussion of theory building in these two sub-areas of curriculum in later chapters.

Theory Implications

Many of the issues and ground rules for theory building around those issues have been laid down in the literature. I conclude this chapter with the following five statements that seem to me to be warranted generalizations so far:

1. Any curriculum theory should begin by defining its set of events.
2. Any curriculum theory should make clear its accepted values and sources for making decisions.
3. Any curriculum theory should specify the characteristics of curriculum design.
4. Any curriculum theory should describe the essential processes for making curriculum decisions and the interrelationships among those processes.
5. Any curriculum theory should provide for continuous regeneration of curriculum decisions.

Such statements are much easier to state than to follow in theory-building work in curriculum, but they can serve as background for amplification of more specific studies and postulations in the following chapters on values, curriculum design, and curriculum engineering.

SUGGESTED READINGS

American Educational Research Association. "Curriculum," *Review of Educational Research*, 39:283-375, June, 1969.
American Educational Research Association. "Curriculum Planning and Development," *Review of Educational Research*, 33:227-337, June, 1963.
American Educational Research Association. "Curriculum Planning and Development," *Review of Educational Research*, 36:339-398, June, 1966.
Anderson, Dan W., James B. Macdonald, and Frank B. May (eds.). *Strategies of Curriculum Development*. Columbus, Ohio: Charles E. Merrill Books, 1965.

Beauchamp, George A. "Basic Components of a Curriculum Theory," *Curriculum Theory Network*, 10:16-22, Fall, 1972.

Beauchamp, George A. *The Curriculum of the Elementary School*. Boston: Allyn and Bacon, Inc., 1964.

Beauchamp, George A. "Curriculum Theory Applied to Urban Schools," *Education in Urban Society*, B.J. Chandler, Lindley J. Stiles, and John I. Kitsuse, editors. New York: Dodd, Mead and Company, 1962, pp. 179-192.

Berman, Louise M. *New Priorities in the Curriculum*. Columbus, Ohio: Charles E. Merrill Publishing Company, 1968.

Broudy, Harry S., B. Othanel Smith, and Joe R. Burnett. *Democracy and Excellence in American Secondary Education*. Chicago: Rand McNally and Company, 1964.

Crary, Ryland W. *Humanizing the School, Curriculum Development and Theory*. New York: Alfred A. Knopf, 1969.

Eisner, Elliot W. (ed.). *Confronting Curriculum Reform*. Boston: Little, Brown and Company, 1971.

Eisner, Elliot W. "Franklin Bobbitt and the 'Science' of Curriculum Making," *The School Review*, 75:29-47, Spring, 1967.

Elliott, David Loucks. *Curriculum Development and History as a Discipline*. Doctor's thesis. New York: Columbia University, 1963.

Faix, Thomas Llewellyn. *Toward a Science of Curriculum: Structural-functional Analysis as a Conceptual System for Theory and Research*. Doctor's thesis. Madison: University of Wisconsin, 1964.

Ford, G.W. and Lawrence Pugno (eds.). *The Structure of Knowledge and the Curriculum*. Chicago: Rand McNally and Company, 1964.

Goodlad, John I., and Maurice N. Richter, Jr. *The Development of a Conceptual System for Dealing with Problems of Curriculum and Instruction*. Los Angeles: Institute for Development of Educational Activities, University of California, 1966.

Goodlad, John I. "The Organizing Center in Curriculum Theory and Practice," *Theory into Practice*, 1:215-221, October, 1962.

Herrick, Virgil E. and Ralph W. Tyler. *Toward Improved Curriculum Theory*. Supplementary Educational Monographs, No. 71. Chicago: The University of Chicago Press, 1950.

Johnson, Mauritz, Jr. "Definitions and Models in Curriculum Theory," *Educational Theory*, 17:127-140, April 1967.

Johnson Mauritz, Jr. "The Translation of Curriculum into Instruction," *Journal of Curriculum Studies*, 1:115-131, May, 1969.

Kirst, Michael W. and Decker F. Walker. "An Analysis of Curriculum Policy-Making," *Review of Educational Research*, 41:479-509, December, 1971.

Klohr, Paul R. "Problems in Curriculum Theory Development," *Theory into Practice*, 6:200-203, October, 1967.

Macdonald, James B. "An Example of Disciplined Curriculum Thinking," *Theory into Practice*, 6:166, October, 1967.

Macdonald, James B. *Some Contributions of a General Behavior Theory for Curriculum*. Doctor's thesis. Madison: University of Wisconsin, 1956.

McClure, Robert M. (ed.). *The Curriculum: Retrospect and Prospect.* The Seventieth Yearbook of the National Society for the Study of Education. Chicago: The University of Chicago Press, 1971.

Parsons, Howard L. "The Humanities and the Curriculum," *Educational Theory*, 11:26-37, January, 1961.

Phillips, Richard Claybourne. "An Historical Study of the Concept Curriculum." Unpublished Ph.D. dissertation, Northwestern University, Evanston, Illinois, 1962.

Robinsohn, Saul B. "A Conceptual Structure of Curriculum Development," *Comparative Education*, 5:221-234, December, 1969.

Rugg, Harold, Chairman. *The Foundations and Technique of Curriculum-Construction.* Twenty-sixth Yearbook of the National Society for the Study of Education, Parts I and II. Bloomington, Ill.: Public School Publishing Company, 1927.

Scott, Harry V. "A Primer of Curriculum Theory: Descriptive Theory," *Educational Theory*, 18:118-124, Spring, 1968.

Seguel, Mary Louise. *The Curriculum Field: Its Formative Years.* New York: Teachers College Press, Columbia University, 1966.

Short, Edmund C. (ed.). "A Search for Valid Content for Curriculum Courses," *Educational Comment/1970.* Toledo, Ohio: College of Education, University of Toledo, 1970.

Smith, B. Othanel, William O. Stanley, and J. Harlan Shores. *Fundamentals of Curriculum Development.* Revised edition. Yonkers-on-Hudson: World Book Company, 1957.

Tyler, Ralph W. *Basic Principles of Curriculum and Instruction.* Syllabus for Education 305. Chicago: The University of Chicago Press, 1950.

Wilson, L. Craig. *The Open Access Curriculum.* Boston: Allyn and Bacon, Inc., 1971.

Witt, Paul W. F. (ed.). *Technology and the Curriculum.* New York: Teachers College Press, 1968.

Chapter 5

VALUES IN CURRICULUM THEORY

Values are products of our culture, generated by both individuals and groups. For us to say that values are important driving forces in the maintenance of the human condition is an understatement. And for an important social institution like the school not to transmit and generate values is incredible. Individuals acquire certain values by a general process of enculturation; they acquire others didactically. The process of schooling employs both approaches.

Values and value judgments permeate curriculum decisions. The primary problem of curriculum is to decide what shall be taught in schools. This is a value question in itself and one that cannot be answered by empirical means. In the process of choosing what shall be taught in schools, a host of additional value judgments must be made. For example, the curriculum simply cannot contain all of the elements of our culture that conceivably might be transmitted to the young. A fundamental process in curriculum planning is that of selecting curriculum content from the total culture; therefore, curriculum planners must address themselves to questions of what knowledge and skills are of most worth and which of those should be included in the curriculum. Curriculum planners have to decide what value concepts are to be taught in schools, and they must decide upon vehicles to be used to help students learn how to deal with value questions. The demand for curriculum attention to values is evidenced by Smith, Stanley, and Shores in the following:

> The heart of a culture is its universals. The heart of the universals is the values or, in other words, the rules by which people order their

social existence. These rules, when built into the personalities of the individuals comprising the society, create the personality type peculiar to the culture. Hence, the heart of any satisfactory educational program consists of those basic values that give meaning to the purposes, plans, and activities of the individual.[1]

In the above sense, value considerations are primarily a problem of curriculum design, but value considerations are also a problem of curriculum engineering. For example, the mustering of values as criteria for determining which curriculum aims and culture content are acceptable in the social-political arena is a necessary task in curriculum planning. But our purpose in this chapter is to develop a rationale for value considerations rather than to expand upon specifics of design and engineering; the latter are the subjects of the following two chapters. First, we take a brief look at some of the ramifications of value interpretations as they generally are presented; we then follow with implications for curriculum theory.

VALUE INTERPRETATIONS

After reviewing various meanings associated with values in the literature, Inlow stated: "Values, to me, simply stated, are the determiners in man that influence his choices in life and that thus decide his behavior."[2] In essence values are the rules by which people shape their behavior. They generally are multi-dimensional. They reflect attitudes or dispositions of individuals to feel and act in given ways. Values embody such concepts as good or bad, homely or pretty, rude or polite, unacceptable or acceptable. Values also involve criteria by which people form dispositions. Kaplan designated a two-way classification when he said, "Values may be distinguished as *instrumental* or *inherent* according to whether they are prized in themselves or because they are believed to lead to something else which we prize."[3] In a similar analysis, Rokeach noted that since values have to do with both modes of conduct and end-states of

---

[1]B. Othanel Smith, William O. Stanley, and J. Harlan Shores, *Fundamentals of Curriculum Development* (revised edition; Yonkers-on-Hudson: World Book Company, 1957), p. 85.

[2]Gail M. Inlow, *Values in Transition* (New York: John Wiley & Sons, Inc., 1972), p. 2.

[3]Abraham Kaplan, *The Conduct of Inquiry* (San Francisco: Chandler Publishing Company, 1964), p. 393.

existence, we may classify values as intrumental or terminal.[4] Industry and honesty are examples of instrumental values; whereas, beauty and freedom are examples of terminal values. Philosophers with differing outlooks or original assumptions tend to interpret values differently. Both Hardie[5] and Park[6] place value theorists in three groups: the intuitive, the skeptical, and pragmatic. Park summarized the three positions as follows:

> The intuitive theory emphasizes the "ultimate" nature of values and man's supposed ability to recognize the ultimate. The skeptic places his emphasis upon the impossibility of moving from beliefs to imperatives. The pragmatist is interested in the existential context in which valuations are made and insists upon determining what is good or bad by probable or actual consequences of acting in terms of a particular judgment.[7]

Whatever the position may be, the general purpose of having a value theory is to provide "a set of guidelines for the meaning and ground of value judgments."[8] Later in the chapter we discuss the implications of value theories for the curriculum theorist; however, the significance of that discussion will be enhanced by looking first into the kinds of questions and problems raised in the area of values.

There seem to be at least two aspects of most value questions. One has to do with the rules for behavior *per se*; the other, with behavioral adaptations to the rules. These two dimensions are expressed in different ways. For example, Frankena distinguished between Moral Education X (MEX) and Moral Education Y (MEY). MEX was used to designate the handing on (through education) of knowledge of good and evil or knowing how to act. MEY referred to education to ensure that individual and group conduct will conform with the knowledge of MEX.[9] Axtelle distinguished between psychological values (matters of fact) and axiological

---

[4]Milton Rokeach, *Beliefs, Attitudes, and Values* (San Francisco: Jossey-Bass, Inc., Publishers, 1970), pp. 159-161.

[5]C. D. Hardie, "The Idea of Value and the Theory of Education," *Educational Theory*, 7:196-199, July, 1957.

[6]Joe Park, "Values and Education," *Education in Urban Society*, edited by B.J. Chandler, Lindley J. Stiles and John I. Kitsuse (New York: Dodd Mead and Company, Inc., 1962), pp. 233-248.

[7]*Ibid.*, p. 242.

[8]Kaplan, *op. cit.*, p. 387.

[9]William K. Frankena, "Toward a Philosophy of Moral Education," *Harvard Educational Review*, 28:300-313, Fall, 1958.

values (what we ought to value).[10] He noted the difference between "the enjoyed and the enjoyable, the desired and the desirable, the satisfying and the satisfactory."[11] Raths, Harmin, and Simon represented such value phenomena as goals, attitudes, feelings, beliefs, interests, and others as value indicators. They termed choosing, prizing, and acting as the processes of valuing.[12] Broudy, Smith, and Burnett proposed that value education has two principal outcomes. One of them is appreciation. The other is the development of strategies for making choices.[13] Whatever the language used may be, there persist two sides of the value question — the value concepts themselves and the processes of human recognition and acceptance of those value concepts as rules for governing behavior.

One gets the general impression from at least certain contemporary literature that the humanistic domain is value-centered whereas the scientific domain is fact-centered. In the bibliography at the end of this chapter, for example, literature is cited bearing such titles as *Humanizing Education*, *The Humanities and the Curriculum*, and *Science and the Humanities*. Basically, the distinctions between humanistic studies and scientific studies have to do with human use and goals. Prior expressed a difference between the final products of scientific activity and humanistic activity as follows:

> . . . the final product of scientific activity is impersonal and uncom-
> mitted in any way to any particular human use or goal; the final
> product of literary effort, on the other hand, is inevitably identified
> with its author's character and his personal artistry, and it cannot
> escape its involvement with particular human feelings and with a
> particular view of human conduct and human aspirations and goals.[14]

Many would take objection to Prior's statement based on grounds that the product may be value-free but the scientist himself is not. Kaplan, for example, points out that it is dubious

---

[10]George E. Axtelle, "The Humanizing of Knowledge and the Education of Values," *Educational Theory*, 16:101-109, April, 1966.

[11]*Ibid.*, p. 107.

[12]Louis E. Raths, Merrill Harmin, and Sidney B. Simon, *Values and Teaching* (Columbus: Charles E. Merrill Books, Inc., 1966), pp. 30-33.

[13]Harry S. Broudy, B. Othanel Smith, and Joe R. Burnett, *Democracy and Excellence in American Secondary Education* (Chicago: Rand McNally and Company, 1964), p. 219.

[14]Moody E. Prior, *Science and the Humanities* (Evanston, Ill.: Northwestern University Press, 1962), p. 17.

whether the scientist actually is concerned only with an impersonal search for truth. He notes that the preponderance of applied research stems from needs for solutions to practical problems.[15] No doubt the argument about the value-free status of the scientist will go on for years to come, but the controversy helps to keep man more conscious of the import of values for his behavior.

Irrespective of this argument, facts and values may be interrelated. Many value statements are supportable by factual evidence. In a discussion of scientific determination of value judgments, Hook stated:

> A scientific or rational approach to judgments of value consists in (a) the investigation of the causes of such judgments, (b) their logical implications, and (c) their probable consequences. This investigation is always to be undertaken in relation to alternative values which limit freedom of choice.[16]

The converse is also tenable. Values become criteria for courses of action leading to empirical information. A teacher who has high regard for rote memoritor learning judges his pupils on evidence from their rote and memoritor performances. Comparably a teacher who places high premium on the more heuristic techniques in learning judges his pupils on evidence of their ability to make observations, to collect information, to use resources, to reach rational generalizations, and so forth. Values so used become principles for guiding action. They first are learned; then they become tools for teaching or for learning.

VALUES AND THE CURRICULUM

Values are a beginning point in curriculum decision making. Goodlad and Richter have proposed that values should be a primary source for selecting school purposes or aims and for all subsequent decisions about the curriculum.[17] In this sense, the values become the criteria for determining the curricular aims. On the other hand, most educational aims are stated as if schools ought

---

[15]*Op. cit.*, p. 389.

[16]Sidney Hook, *Education for Modern Man* (new edition: Alfred A. Knopf, 1963), p. 179.

[17]John I. Goodlad and Maurice N. Richter, Jr., "The Development of a Conceptual System for Dealing with Problems of Curriculum and Instruction," Report of an inquiry supported by the Cooperative Research Program of the Office of Education, U. S. Department of Health, Education, and Welfare, Contract No. SAE - 8024, Project No. 454, 1966.

to accomplish designated ends. The aims thus are statements of
value judgment in themselves. For example, we may state that an
aim of the secondary school is to improve citizenship. In value
terms, we would be averring that the improvement of citizenship
behavior is worthwhile and that the school ought to do something
about it. Note that the statement includes no attempt to describe
citizenship behavior, and therefore, it gives no direction for the
teaching of citizenship behaviors nor for the measuring of the
effects of the teaching. In this circumstance, it is apparent that the
generalized aim needs to be translated into the language of
curriculum strategy and instructional strategy. The translation of
aims into curriculum strategy and instructional strategy becomes
the means of the ends-means continuum.

It is in the realm of aim declaration that much of our modern
controversy lies with respect to values. One may state that an aim of
schooling is to teach the young to be literate, that is, to teach them to
read and write their language. This aim is only value laden at the
points of deciding that this imposition should be made upon
children and that this function should be carried out by schools
rather than by some other agency of society. Conversely, for one to
state that an aim of schooling is to foster an ideal of a common
human community or to develop a rugged individualistic and
nationalistic spirit is heavily value laden. Educational planners
have had success in developing curricular and instructional
strategies as means for achieving the ends of the literacy aim, but
few have done anything with the latter.

As we indicated earlier, some values are acquired by the young
through the processes of general enculturation. Others have to be
taught. Very frequently, the values acquired through general
enculturation are in conflict with those selected to be taught in
schools. Some very vivid examples are occurring in our
communities today, and not all of them in large urban
communities. One of these is the values implied by the open
hostility of certain ethnic and/or religious groups toward blacks
and other minority groups. Yet most of the persons who exhibit
such hostility would profess that they believe in the equality of man
and in equality of opportunity for all mankind, and on Sunday
mornings in churches, they routinely avow to believe in the
brotherhood of man. The purpose here is to illustrate that many

attempts on the part of schools to affect significantly the value orientations of their pupils may run counter to the forces of enculturation.

Stating Behavioral Objectives

In much curriculum literature, a distinction is made between the general aims of education and the specific behavioral objectives to be fostered by the systems of schooling. If curriculum planners wish to include specific behavioral objectives in their curriculum, a major task for them is the stating, classifying, and arranging of the behavioral objectives within the curriculum. It is commonplace for us to say that behavioral objectives fall into three categories: the cognitive, the psychomotor, and the affective. The three actually are applicable to any subject, but they have different weightings from subject to subject. Our concern at the moment is mostly with the affective domain. In this connection, some guidelines for the curriculum planner are available even though they come from a single source. The publication, *A Taxonomy of Educational Objectives, Handbook II: Affective Domain* classifies value objectives into five categories in ascending complexity. The following is a condensation of the taxonomical structure for affective behaviors listed in that publication:

1.0 Receiving (attending)
    1.1 Awareness
    1.2 Willingness to receive
    1.3 Controlled or selected attention
2.0 Responding
    2.1 Acquiescence in responding
    2.2 Willingness to respond
    2.3 Satisfaction in response
3.0 Valuing
    3.1 Acceptance of a value
    3.2 Preference for a value
    3.3 Commitment
4.0 Organization
    4.1 Conceptualization of a value
    4.2 Organization of a value system
5.0 Characterization by a value or value complex
    5.1 Generalized set
    5.2 Characterization[18]

---

[18]David R. Krathwohl, Benjamin S. Bloom, and Bertram B. Masia, *A Taxonomy of Educational Objectives, Handbook II: Affective Domain* (New York: David McKay Company, Inc., 1964), pp. 176-185.

Taking his cue from the taxonomies, Johnson arranged a schema for curriculum. Under that portion classifying learning outcomes, he listed knowledge, techniques, and values as three classes of outcomes. Under values, he listed two sub-classes: (1) norms — societal prescriptions and preferences regarding belief and conduct and (2) predilections — individual preferential dispositions (attitudes, interests, appreciations, aversions).[19]

When taxonomies contribute meaningfully to classification, they materially aid the curriculum planner with details of arrangement of curriculum content. They also aid in the development of appraisal instruments. But taxonomies do not help materially with the tasks of selecting values and beliefs to be included in the curriculum. At the moment, two avenues seem available to curriculum planners, and they have been identified earlier in this chapter. One is to search the recognized school subjects and the scholarly disciplines for value content that reflects decisions made in earlier times. The other is to make judgments about existing values in the general culture ethos of the school and its community. The selection of values is very much a judgmental procedure, and curriculum planners must face up to the task in that light.

Values as Curriculum Content

Most of the foregoing discussion in this chapter leads to the conclusion that values direct the character of school aims, but additionally values are a part of the culture content of the curriculum. It goes without saying that values as curriculum content would include value concepts as knowledge of rules of behavior and the processes of dealing with value considerations that may or may not lead to personal acceptance of value concepts as self-governing rules for behavior. This dual interpretation of values as content may be thought of as a curricular interpretation of the two-way classification of values as terminal, or end-state of existence, values and instrumental values, or it may be thought of as a curricular application of the distinction between the value concepts themselves and the processes of value clarification as

---

[19]Mauritz Johnson, Jr., "Definitions and Models in Curriculm Theory," *Educational Theory*, 17:138, April, 1967.

previously described. In any case, curriculum planners face the problem of distinguishing between values as substantive curriculum content and the processes of valuing as curriculum content.

Probably the first task of curriculum planners with respect to values as curriculum content is to identify and state those attitudes, beliefs, ideals, or concepts that are to be included in the curriculum. O'Connor suggested that these should consist of "a set of values or ideals embodied and expressed in the purposes for which knowledge, skills, and attitudes are imparted. . . ."[20] He indicated that such values might be classified in five categories: (1) minimum skills, (2) vocational training, (3) awakening the desire for knowledge, (4) developing a critical outlook, and (5) the appreciation of human achievements.[21] Broudy, Smith, and Burnett stated: "Three kinds of norms should be taken into account as the content of the curriculum is selected. These are the norms of efficiency or prescriptive rules, regulatory norms, and moral norms."[22] In acknowledging that the values of any society are embedded in its culture, Smith, Stanley, and Shores identified three elements in which the core of the American value system lies — the democratic tradition, the belief in the maximum development of the individual, and the institutions established to perpetuate the values.[23] Inlow indicated the rationalist tradition, the Judeo-Christian ethic, the Anglo-Saxon Tradition and pragmatic faith as the major sources of the values of the western world, particularly the United States.[24] A very practical, and often overlooked, source of value content for curriculum planners is the ethos of the community the school is destined to serve. The values that drive the inhabitants of a racial ghetto are vastly different from those of the inhabitants of a wealthy suburb. Value concepts considered acceptable in one community are not in others. Witness, for example, the problems experienced with attempts to include sex education in the curricula for elementary and secondary schools, or the conflicts that have arisen over the celebration of religious holidays in schools.

---

[20]*Op. cit.*, p. 5.
[21]*Ibid.*, pp. 8-13.
[22]*Op. cit.*, p. 150.
[23]*Op. cit., pp. 76-82.*
[24]*Op. cit.*, p. 20.

Something that is often overlooked in curriculum work is that the very choice of subjects for a school is a value choice. It is assumed, for example, that the choice of seven, eight, or nine subjects for elementary schools will provide the general-education type program believed to be essential for children of elementary-school age. It is also loosely assumed that the use of those subjects as the organizational framework for the educational program will fulfill the overall aims of education for children in the society.

Unquestionably, statements of aims do not lead directly to the selection of school subjects as means for attaining those aims. The aims, by definition, imply that schools should be instrumental in achieving certain ends. There ought to be a criteria relationship between the aims and the subjects selected to advance them, but there too seldom is. Both curriculum theorists and curriculum planners need to examine this problem more critically.

Within most, if not all, school subjects, there are value components. Phenix classified the realms of meaning as symbolics, empirics, esthetics, synnoetics, ethics, and synoptics.[25] Some, if not all, of these realms are value sources. The humanities and the social studies are considered to be important sources for values. All of the disciplines have unique groups of value concepts. All have their own modes of behaving and classes of problem. Nevertheless, there is a great deal of difference in the value load of subjects like music or literature and mathematics or physics.

It would be disastrous for curriculum planners to attempt to include in a curriculum all of the possible value concepts that might be identified in our culture. Such an attempt would be akin to searching for gold in a bottomless pit. Planners will be forced to be selective and include specifically those value concepts that they deem to have high priority and community acceptance. There may be certain precepts of nationalism, rules for human conduct, or principles of democracy that planners will wish to include in the curriculum, but what they must insure is that an opportunity is provided for students to test, examine, and explore the endorsed values as well as those that arise that are not endorsed.

As previously indicated, Raths, Harmin, and Simon identified

---

[25]Philip H. Phenix, *Realms of Meaning* (New York: McGraw-Hill Book Company, 1964).

choosing, prizing, and acting as the processes of valuing. Coombs listed the following as objectives of value analysis:

1. Teaching students to rate a value object in a particular way.
2. Helping students to make the most rational judgment they can make about the value object in question.
3. Teaching students to make rational value judgments.
4. Teaching students how to operate as members of a group attempting to come to a common value judgment about some value object.[26]

The inquiry processes implied by these objectives are processes of valuing. So are such processes as accepting, thinking, criticizing, testing, judging and reasoning. Others could be added to the list. The point is that these processes are just as much curriculum content as the concept "honesty," and they should be treated as such. The processes may be more important as curriculum content than are the concepts because the concepts become clarified through exercise of the processes. Since values and valuing are not normally a separate subject in the school curriculum, they emerge from the study of all cultural elements whether they be labeled a discipline, problems of living, or persistent life situations. The processes of valuing therefore must be made a part of a total curriculum strategy to be most effective.

IMPLICATIONS FOR CURRICULUM THEORY BUILDING

All of the implications of value theories, values themselves, and processes of valuing for theory building in curriculum are not clearly evident. Nevertheless, one has to assume that the acceptance of different value theories would lead to differences in curriculum theories. On the other hand, a case could be made that value theories are also applicable in passing judgment upon curriculum theories. In the absence of clearly stated curriculum theories, it is difficult to test out either assumption scientifically.

To illustrate the difficulties, we might examine where in the work of the curriculum theorist, an assumption of a given value theory might affect his work. One of the most important functions of a value theory is to establish bases, or criteria, for determining what is "good." The intuitive value theorist typically asserts that

---

[26]Jerrold R. Coombs, "Objectives of Value Analysis," *Values Education*, Forty-first Yearbook of the National Council for the Social Studies, ed. Lawrence E. Metcalf (Washington: the Council, 1971), p. 19.

ideas and principles (values) exist in their own right and that man can become aware of them by the process of intuition. Once aware of them he can use them to guide his own behavior. One who holds pragmatic value theory judges value concepts and principles according to the degree to which they lead to satisfactory consequences. The notion of "goodness" in this case is determined by observation of what people do that brings them satisfaction in life.

Two implications seem to emerge for the curriculum theorist from such variation in value outlook. One implication is for the input information for a curriculum system. What shall be the sources of values to be used as influence upon the work of the curriculum planner? If the theorist chooses the intuitive position, his sources tend to be those that reveal permanent and universal values such as the word of a church, the wisdom of the ancient scholars, or the word of political bodies. If the curriculum theorist chooses the pragmatic position, he is more contextualist; his sources for values are the rules for satisfactory living in the culture in which the school lies. The processes of determining them are observation and experimentation.

A second implication is for the choice of value content to be included in the curriculum. What knowledge about values is to be transmitted to the young through schools? How can that knowledge be most effectively organized as part of the curriculum? What processes for dealing with value problems will the school stress? How shall statements about these processes be arranged in the curriculum so as to lead to the development of effective instructional strategies? Such questions are imperative if curriculum planners are to correct their previous failure to identify the package, or packages, of values the schools are attempting to make an integral part of the educational program. The consequences of the two value theories used here as examples would affect all the questions raised, and they should be apparent from the foregoing discussions. Briefly then, different value theory orientation would influence the work of the curriculum theorist at two points — his treatment of input data for a curriculum system and his treatment of curriculum design.

Value theories and the values derived therefrom can be instrumental in judging the worth of the work of a curriculum theorist as well as in affecting the character of the work. For example, a task for the curriculum theorist is to explain relationships between statements of aims for schooling and the selection of culture content as a means for achieving the aims. A curriculum planning group may state its aims and select a body of culture content. In essence, what the group does is to predict that if the culture content is developed properly through the instructional environment, the aims will be achieved. The theorist must explain this relationship and its ramifications. Many stated aims are value statements exclusively. Others are statements of principle to be used to direct behavior. The latter, in particular, can be used to judge the effectiveness of the theorist's explanation and predictions as well as the predictive operations of the practitioner.

SUMMARY

The implications of values and value theories for curriculum theory have not been explored to the present time in depth. Most, in fact, concede that curriculum planners and other educators have failed to deal with the subject of values adequately for modern schooling. As a consequence, it has been necessary in this chapter for us to explore some of the implications of values and value theories for selected practical aspects of curriculum so that the theoretical implications might be inferred.

At least two dimensions of values have import for a curriculum. The first consists of value concepts and generalizations that may be classified as substantive knowledge. The second is more syntactical; it consists of the processes by which students will learn to cope with value problems and to come to accept values as rules governing their own behavior.

Value theorists have been classified into three groups: the intuitive, the skeptic, and the pragmatic. Each value position has its unique way of identifying and verifying value judgments. Presumably, each would have a different impact upon the work of the curriculum theorists and the practitioner. We may assume that acceptance of one value theory over others would produce uniqueness in a curriculum theory. We also may assume that the acceptance of one value theory over others would uniquely affect judgments made about curriculum theories.

SUGGESTED READINGS

"A Symposium: What can Philosophy Contribute to Educational Theory?" *Harvard Educational Review*, 28:283-339, Fall, 1958.

Axtelle, George E. "The Humanizing of Knowledge and the Education of Values," *Educational Theory*, 16:101-109, April, 1966.

Barr, Robert D., (ed.). *Values and Youth*. National Council for the Social Studies. Washington, D.C., 1971.

Bayles, Ernest E. "Are Values Verifiable?" *Educational Theory*, 10:71-77, January, 1960.

Beck, Clive. *Moral Education in the Schools*. The Ontario Institute for Studies in Education. Ontario, Canada, 1971.

Berman, Louise M. (ed.). *The Humanities and the Curriculum*. Washington: Association for Supervision and Curriculum Development, NEA, 1967.

Broudy, Harry S., B. Othanel Smith, and Joe R. Burnett. *Democracy and Excellence in American Secondary Education*. Chicago: Rand McNally and Company, 1964.

Bruner, Jerome S. *On Knowing*. Cambridge: The Belknap Press of Harvard University Press, 1963.

Educational Policies Commission. *The Central Purpose of American Education*. Washington: the Commission, 1961.

Goals for Americans. A Report of the President's Commission on National Goals. Englewood Cliffs: Prentice-Hall, Inc., 1960.

Goss, Charles E. "A Critique of the Ethical Aspects of Phenix's Curriculum Theory," *Educational Theory*, 17:40-47, January, 1967.

Hardie, C.D. "The Idea of Value and the Theory of Education," *Educational Theory*, 7:196-199, July, 1957.

Hare, R.M. *The Language of Morals*. Oxford: The Clarendon Press, 1952.

Hook, Sidney. *Education for Modern Man*. New edition. New York: Alfred A. Knopf, 1963.

Hutchins, Robert M. *The Conflict in Education in a Democratic Society*. New York: Harper and Brothers, 1953.

Krathwohl, David R., Benjamin S. Bloom, and Bertram B. Masia. *A Taxonomy of Educational Objectives*, Handbook II: Affective Domain. New York: David McKay Company, Inc., 1964.

Metcalf, Lawrence E. (ed.). *Values Education: Rationale Strategies and Procedures*. Washington, D.C.: National Council for the Social Studies, 1971.

Myrdal, Gunnar. *Value in Social Theory*. New York: Harper & Brothers, 1958.

O'Connor, D.J. *An Introduction to the Philosophy of Education*. London: Routledge and Kegan Paul, 1957.

Park, Joe. "Values and Education," *Education in Urban Society*, edited by B.J. Chandler, Lindley J. Stiles, and John I. Kitsuse. New York: Dodd Mead and Company, Inc., 1962, pp. 233-248.

Phenix, Philip H. *Realms of Meaning*. New York: McGraw-Hill Book Company, 1964.

Prior, Moody E. *Science and the Humanities*. Evanston, Ill.: Northwestern University Press, 1962.

Raths, Louis E., Merrill Harmin, and Sidney B. Simon. *Values and Teaching.* Columbus: Charles E. Merrill Books, Inc., 1966.

Rokeach, Milton. *Beliefs, Attitudes and Values.* San Francisco: Jossey-Bass, Inc., Publishers, 1970.

Simon, Sidney B., W. Leland Howe, and Howard Kirschenbaum. *Values Clarification.* New York: Hart Publishing Co., 1972.

Smith, B. Othanel, William O. Stanley, and J. Harlan Shores. *Fundamentals of Curriculum Development.* Revised edition. Yonkers-on-Hudson: World Book Company, 1957.

Smith, Philip G. (ed.). *Theories of Value and Problems of Education.* Chicago: University of Illinois Press, 1970.

Wilhelms, Fred T. "Humanization Via the Curriculum," *Humanizing Education: the Person in the Process,* edited by Robert R. Leeper. Washington: Association for Supervision and Curriculum Development, NEA, 1967, pp. 19-32.

Chapter 6

CURRICULUM DESIGN

Earlier, it was established that the word *curriculum* is used in three ways: (1) as a curriculum, (2) as the name of a system of schooling, and (3) as a title of a field of study. Further, curriculum theory was depicted as containing two primary dimensions, or sub-theories: curriculum design and curriculum engineering. Curriculum design may be defined as the substance and organization of goals and culture content so arranged as to reveal potential progression through levels of schooling. Since decisions in the field of curriculum, including curriculum engineering, hinge directly upon the curriculum, curriculum design is the focal point of virtually all curriculum thinking. From a theoretical point of view, curriculum design theory should constitute the most critical sub-theory of curriculum theory.

In this chapter, we shall expand upon the practical and theoretical issues and problems of curriculum design that force one to the conclusion that curriculum design theory must be a unique sub-theory of curriculum theory. The chapter is divided into three sections. In the first section, we shall examine the meanings associated with curriculum design, in the second section the problems of the substantive elements of a curriculum, and in the third section options for content arrangement.

DESIGN DEFINITIONS

The theoretical issues associated with the concept of curriculum as a document (as a curriculum, that is) fall under the heading of *curriculum design*. Curriculum design was defined above as the substance and organization of goals and culture content so arranged as to reveal potential progression through levels of schooling. According to Taba:

> Curriculum design is a statement which identifies the elements of the curriculum, states what their relationships are to each other, and indicates the principles of organization and the requirement of that organization for the administrative conditions under which it is to operate.[1]

Johnson identified three notions of curriculum design as:

(a) An arrangement of selected and ordered learning outcomes intended to be achieved through instruction,

(b) An arrangement of selected and ordered learning experiences to be provided in an instructional situation, and

(c) A scheme for planning and providing learning experiences.[2]

However one may conceptualize curriculum design, it is the design characteristics that make one curriculum like or different from another.

There commonly are two fundamental dimensions of curriculum design. The first has to do with the total substance, the elements and the arrangement of the document. We may speak of these as the contents of a curriculum in the same sense that we use a table of contents for a book to specify the titles of the various chapters. The second is the mode of organization of the various parts of a curriculum, particularly the culture content. Both of these dimensions circumscribe subordinate parts. We should keep in mind that the technical terms and statements used to describe a curriculum constitute the theoretical language of curriculum design. The focus of language to explain curriculum design is upon the two dimensions. Each of these merits full discussion because they are so critical to curriculum theory and research.

THE ELEMENTS OF A CURRICULUM

Literature on curriculum is replete with discussions about definitions of curriculum, curriculum decision-making,

---

[1]Hilda Taba, *Curriculum Development: Theory and Practice* (New York: Harcourt, Brace, and World, Inc., 1962), p. 421.

[2]Mauritz Johnson, Jr. "On the Meaning of Curriculum Design," *Curriculum Theory Network*, 3:5, Spring, 1969.

curriculum planning, curriculum strategy, and so forth, but very little of it describes the finished product, or the output, of such endeavor. In other words, organized descriptions of curriculum designs are not plentiful. For many years, I have insisted that a curriculum is a written document. This point of view, when countered, is usually challenged by statements to the effect that the curriculum is not a written document or that it is "more than" a written document. What the curriculum is, if it is not a written document, or exactly what in it rises above a written document, those taking a stand do not make clear. Others claim that the written curriculum is not the "real curriculum." Again, what constitutes the "real curriculum" is not made clear. But regardless of interpretation, if a curriculum is something that is planned, it must be composed of elements with form and structure.

Design and Schooling

Conceivably, it will be helpful for us to look at some of the dynamics of the schooling situation for cues for curriculum design features. Important social institutions like schools may be justified only in terms of the goals or purposes they are intended to serve. Once goals are recognized and accepted, means must be selected for the attainment of the goals. Let us use Figure 6 as a model for illustrating these conditions for schools. In the figure, the goals lead to the selection of means to be used in achieving those goals. Two classes of means are indicated for schools. One of them is a curriculum; the other is instruction that takes place in response to the curriculum. The processes of evaluation help us to determine the adequacy of the two means in producing the desired results. The achievement of the goals and the results of evaluation help us

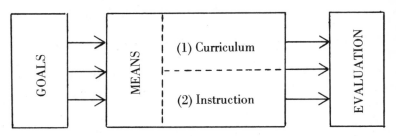

Figure 6. *The dynamic cycle of schooling.*

to redefine the goals and replan the means for achieving them. Thus, a dynamic cycle is established for the planning of schooling functions.

This kind of reasoning, however, immediately indicates two subsystems of schooling labeled curriculum and instruction, and this very designation of curriculum and instruction as two categories instead of one is another source of confusion. Related to these categories are the purposes of having a curriculum in the first place, and it is here that the theorist must bring the relationships between curriculum and instruction into focus. What the contents of a curriculum are depends entirely upon whether both curriculum strategy and instructional strategy are to be encompassed in the curriculum design, and there does not seem to be any way of avoiding this decision. For investigators to theorize and conduct relevant research, their language and constructs have to be carefully ordered. It is rational for the two means of achieving the ends of schooling to be conceived as two separate but related strategies. One set is conceptualized around the answers reached in response to the question, "What shall we teach in the school(s)?" The expression of those answers may be termed the curriculum, and their form and arrangement the curriculum design. The second set, the instructional strategies, is conceptualized around individual teachers and groups of pupils in response to the general question, "How shall we teach?" A sequence of events running from the development of curriculum strategy, to the development of instructional strategy, to the actual activities of pupils in classrooms or elsewhere is thus a logical one. None of these strategies is pupil learnings. These rather take place as a result of the strategies and events. In fact, curriculum designers should plan only in anticipation of learning activities and outcomes. In contrast, curriculum theorists or workers who think of curriculum strategy, instructional strategy, and/or actual classroom activities as constituting a single ball of wax called curriculum, pose an entirely different problem in curriculum design. Curriculum and schooling become almost the same concept. Curriculum design then includes an arrangement of objectives, subject matter chosen, specific action plans for teaching, all forms of instructional materials to be used, time schedules, activity descriptions, and so forth. If one goes further and includes what pupils learn as part of curriculum, the many components of evaluation also have to be added. In fact, it is difficult to conceptualize what a curriculum design would look like in such a scheme.

Elements Implied by Definition of Curriculum

Virtually all writers on the subject of curriculum have been compelled to define curriculum. There is much variance in the ways curriculum is defined even though subsequent discussion may be quite similar. This variance reveals itself in the following samples of selected definitions. Buswell used the term to mean "whatever content is used purposely by the school as a stimulus to learning."[3] Smith, Stanley and Shores stated:

> A sequence of potential experiences is set up in the school for the purpose of disciplining children and youth in group ways of thinking and acting. This set of experiences is referred to as the *curriculum*.[4]

For Inlow, curriculum "is that body of value-goal-oriented learning content, existing as a written document or in the minds of teachers, that, when energized by instruction, results in change in pupil behavior."[5] Wilson defined curriculum as "a planned set of human encounters thought to maximize learning."[6] Doll concluded that: "The curriculum is now generally considered to be all of the experiences that learners have under the auspices or direction of the school."[7] Firth and Kimpston state that "The curriculum is a vital, moving, complex interaction of people and things in a fluid setting. It encompasses questions to be debated, forces to be rationalized, goals to be illuminated, programs to be activated, and outcomes to be evaluated."[8] Ragan used the term curriculum "to include all of the experiences for which the school accepts responsibility."[9] Faunce and Bossing gave a similar

---

[3]G.T. Buswell, "Organization and Sequence of the Curriculum," *The Psychology of Learning*, National Society for the Study of Education Forty-first Yearbook, Part II (Bloomington, Ill.: Public School Publishing Company, 1942), p. 446.

[4]B. Othanel Smith, William O. Stanley, and J. Harlan Shores, *Fundamentals of Curriculum Development* (revised edition; Harcourt, Brace, and World, Inc., 1957), p.3.

[5]Gail M. Inlow, *The Emergent in Curriculum* (2d ed.; New York: John Wiley & Sons, Inc., 1973), p. 41.

[6]L. Craig Wilson, *The Open Access Curriculum* (Boston: Allyn and Bacon, Inc., 1971), p. 64.

[7]Ronald C. Doll, *Curriculum Improvement: Decision-Making and Process* (2d ed.; Boston: Allyn and Bacon, Inc., 1970), p. 24.

[8]Gerald R. Firth and Richard D. Kimpston, *The Curricular Continuum in Perspective* (Itasca, Ill.: F.E. Peacock Publishers, Inc., 1973), p. 3.

[9]William B. Ragan and G. D. Sheperd, *Modern Elementary Curriculum* (4th ed.; New York: Holt, Rinehart and Winston, Inc., 1971), p.3.

definition.[10] Wagner stated that "Whatever it is that a child learns under the guidance and direction of the school is 'his' curriculum."[11] Others have held a similar point of view. Hopkins indicated that each child makes his own curriculum from the school environment.[12] Miel made a distinction between the curriculum of each child and the old curriculum, or the course of study.[13] It is interesting to note here that Foshay attributed the many interpretations of curriculum after 1930 to a single basic idea, which was the concept of experience promulgated by John Dewey.[14] Such variation in definition led Beauchamp to conclude that there have been represented in the literature three discrete sets of associations with the concept curriculum; namely, the experience notion, the social design notion, and the psychological notion.[15] Even though the discreteness of these differences has not been elaborated, one must conclude that the existence of difference in definition should set the stage for differences in curriculum design and in curriculum theory.

All of this argument about meanings associated with curriculum is centered in two basic ideas. We have already presented one in depicting curriculum differentially as a curriculum, a curriculum system, and a field of study. The number and complexity of the referents here contribute to confusion in communication. The second, and probably the real fly in the ointment, is the word *experiences.* Most attempts in recent decades at defining curriculum focus on the concept of experience. The key phrase in almost all definitions of curriculum is *experience* or *learning experience.* The use of the term originated with the philosophic notion of experience in the sense expressed by John Dewey. For an individual to have an experience, Dewey insisted that it would be necessary for the learner to engage himself in

---

[10]Roland C. Faunce and Nelson L. Bossing, *Developing the Core Curriculum* (2d ed.; Englewood Cliffs: Prentice-Hall, Inc., p. 115.

[11]Guy Wagner, "A Present Day Look at the American School Curriculum," *Education*, 78:328, February, 1958.

[12]L.T. Hopkins, "Who Makes the Curriculum?" *Teachers College Record*, 52:277, February, 1951.

[13]Alice M. Miel, "The School Curriculum in a Changing Culture,"*Education Digest*, 21:21, November, 1955.

[14]Arthur W. Foshay, "Changing Interpretations of the Elementary Curriculum," *The American Elementary School*, Thirteenth Yearbook of the John Dewey Society, edited by Harold G. Shane (New York: Harper and Brothers, 1953), p. 17.

[15]George A. Beauchamp, "Curriculum Organization and Development in Historical Perspective," *Review of Educational Research*, 27:245, June, 1957.

activities from which he can learn something that he has not learned before. In addition, through that activity he must recognize and foresee the consequences of that learning for his present and future behavior. This action establishes continuity within the life experience of the individual and gives meaning to his actions. Obviously, the significant psychological process by which an individual thus acquires experience is critical or reflective thinking. In order for an individual to have an experience in this sense, then, the learner must see the utility and consequence of his learning in the broad perspective of life. The concept of experience thus conceived is not something one plans. The best that can be done is to create environments in which individuals hopefully will have experiences. Only the learner can have a learning experience. The task of the curriculum planner is to establish the basic structure for an environment in which the learners *may have* learning experiences. The curriculum planner can only anticipate the conditions under which learners may have learning experiences. Another use of experience seems to be as a substitute for the word *activity*, but when this is the case, the curriculum planner may, if he wishes, consider the setting forth of an array of activities as part of the curriculum being designed. Communication among curriculum workers would probably be greatly clarified and facilitated if the use of the word *experience* were discontinued in our curriculum literature, particularly at the level of definition.

Document Features

For the remainder of this discussion of the elements of a curriculum, it is assumed that a curriculum is a written document. In this frame of reference, design features, or curriculum contents and their arrangements, are easily envisioned. A commonly included feature is an outline of the culture content to be taught. These statements, whether long or brief, usually are arranged sequentially by grades, or levels, according to the administrative organization of the school for which the curriculum is intended. A subsequent section of this chapter will be devoted entirely to this topic; thus here it will be left as one of the ingredients of a curriculum albeit a major one.

Another component that is frequently included in a curriculum is a statement of goals and/or specific objectives. These may range from statements of overall purpose of a school to very highly specific cognitive, psychomotor, and affective changes in behavior sought through the efforts of a school. The same curriculum may contain a generalized statement of purposes for schooling in an introductory section and specific objectives in a second section in which the culture content is described. One can find curriculums that contain only a statement of outcomes. The position taken by Johnson would foster essentially this idea.[16] It will be recalled that to Johnson a curriculum is a set of intended learning outcomes. Johnson would include in the curriculum, in addition to the intended learning outcomes, rules for moving from the set of intended outcomes into the instructional domain, but he would relegate the choice of and organization of culture content to those who are to plan the curriculum. By definition, Goodlad and Richter ostensibly would agree with Johnson when they state that "a curriculum is a set of intended learnings."[17] For them, intended learnings are end products that are a consequence of education. This language is the language of educational goals or objectives, and thus approximates the point of view of Johnson.

A third ingredient that may be included in a curriculum is a statement that sets forth the purposes for the creation of the curriculum and that stipulates the ways in which the curriculum is to be used. The most obvious need is for designers to state in straightforward language the relationships between the curriculum and the development of instructional strategies. The general process of moving from the planned curriculum to instruction is called curriculum implementation. Such statements in a curriculum may be thought of as a set of rules for implementation. Another possibility for inclusion would be a description of the contents and organization of the curriculum and the purposes for including each. A statement about the way in which the curriculum was planned, and how it is to be appraised and reconstructed, is generally warranted. The statement has most

---

[16]Mauritz Johnson, Jr., "Definitions and Models in Curriculum Theory," *Educational Theory*, 17:127-140, April, 1967.

[17]John I. Goodlad and Maurice N. Richter, Jr., *The Development of a Conceptual System for Dealing with Problems of Curriculum and Instruction* (Los Angeles: Institute for Development of Educational Activities, University of California, 1966), pp. 11-12.

value as an initial statement in the curriculum. It facilitates the system of curriculum engineering.

A fourth possible item for inclusion in a curriculum, and one that is rarely included, is an appraisal scheme. The appraisal scheme is a plan for determining the adequacy and worth of the curriculum and for identifying the intended contribution of the various parts to it. For example, if the curriculum is intended to be used as a point of departure for all teachers in the development of their instructional strategies, whether or not they use it, and how well they use the curriculum for these purposes is the first place to bring the appraisal processes to bear. Another possibility is to test, through the appraisal scheme, any correlation between intended learning outcomes and learnings actually measured or observed subsequent to instruction. Since an appraisal scheme by definition furnishes data about the success and worth of the curriculum, the data becomes feedback information for reconstituting the curriculum contents and usage.

These four items appear to be reasonable for inclusion as parts of a curriculum. All curriculums include at least one of them. There may be other items that are included, but they probably would fall under the general umbrella of one or more of these four, unless the curriculum entries pertain to instructional matters. The next section contains a broadened description of issues in connection with the organization of culture content because most of the contemporary discussion about curriculum design falls under that general heading.

CULTURE CONTENT IN A CURRICULUM

In the previous section, it was pointed out that some curriculum theorists believe that a curriculum should singularly consist of statements of school objectives or intended learning outcomes. Others, on the other hand, insist that a curriculum is more than a statement of objectives. They would hold that curriculum planners should make the initial selection of cultural content that they feel would aid in the attainment of the objectives. I use the term *culture content* to avoid argument about interpretations of such phases as subject matter, content, or any other term that might be used. Culture content may be thought of as two kinds. One is that culture content that is systematically organized in what we have come to know as the disciplines, particularly those disciplines wherein certain knowledge or skill is prerequisite to other knowledge attainment. Practical knowledge may be distinguished from the disciplines in that it has not been organized and systematically treated by scholars to the same extent that the disciplines have. In fact, great debates have ensued over the distinction between discipline knowledge and practical knowledge particularly with respect to the role of the school. Some would hold that the school should only be concerned with discipline knowledge and not at all with practical knowledge. Whereas, other persons would hold that practical knowledge has great worth. Commonly, the elementary school program is composed mostly of practical knowledge, the high school a little of both, and the college principally discipline knowledge.

Organization Patterns

Historically, most of the argument about curriculum design has been connected with the organization of culture content within a curriculum. Most curriculum books contain some reference to types of curriculum that acquired their names from their design characteristics. Most readers will be familiar with such displays in the language of the separate subjects curriculum, the correlated curriculum, the broad fields curriculum, the activity curriculum, the problems of living curriculum, the persistent life situations curriculum, the core curriculum, the experience curriculum, the emergent curriculum. Supposedly, each of these call for a different arrangement of the culture content. It is fair to say that most of these curriculums tended to move away from a separate subject approach toward some pattern believed to facilitate learning on the part of the pupils. The fundamental argument was over the logical versus the psychological organization of the subject matter or culture content. On the one hand, proponents of logical organization contended that school subjects had their own internal organization and that curriculum planners should create curriculum designs that would capitalize upon the logical orderliness of the subject. Advocates of psychological organization of subject matter emphasize an organization allegedly designed to facilitate learning by pupils because the organization aided pupils in the integration of culture content from several or all of the school subjects or by providing integrated units of work irrespective of school subject.

All are familiar with the great revival of interest in curriculum beginning around mid-century. The combined effect of critics of school practices, the availability of foundational and government grants of money for the study of education, and an upsurge of interest in problems of curriculum and instruction by scholars from the various disciplines produced a rash of curriculum activity. These were illustrated by the Biological Sciences Curriculum Study, the School Mathematics Study Group, and Project Social Studies, to mention only a few. It is most interesting to note that in the more recent developments, direction of change is completely opposite to that of the earlier period. In the earlier period, attempts were made to move away from a separate subject or discipline-centered scheme of organization toward an organization in which the individual subjects would lose their separate identities by being combined, for instance, into language arts, social studies, core, persistent life situations, or problems of living designs. The more recent innovations have stressed a return to the organizational features of the individual disciplines and to more careful programming of each discipline according to its own characteristics and rules. Furthermore, most of the newly developed designs have been characterized as curriculum innovations even though they are concerned exclusively with single subjects such as mathematics, chemistry, or English. Little or no attention is given to the interrelationships among the various subjects, nor do the designers give evidence of realizing that a curriculum is something that has to characterize a whole school program. This is a very important distinction. I would hold the view that there is no such thing as a mathematics curriculum or a social studies curriculum. A curriculum is a plan for a school, and as a result, it must contain an organization of all of the culture content selected for the school. Furthermore, the organization must depict the relationships among the various designated parts of the culture content.

School organization also has a great deal of influence upon

design features of curriculum. It is easier to talk about the whole curriculum and/or the fusion of subjects in elementary schools where the organizational pattern has conventionally been the self-contained classroom, or more recently a nongraded organization, than in the departmentalized multiteacher organization of the secondary schools. Many of our preconceived notions about curriculum design may have to change drastically under the stimulation of such features as team teaching and nongraded units. But one cannot help wondering which comes first — administrative organization patterns like nongradedness and modular scheduling or a curriculum design. Many textbooks on professional education boldly state that we first must decide upon what kind of curriculum we wish to carry out in our schools before determining a pattern of organization for the school. So far, differences between a curriculum designed for a graded school and a nongraded school are few in number; customarily, portions of the same curriculum are assigned to the variously constituted groups. Irrespective of this state of affairs, it is important to note that a principle in curriculum design is that the design and the organizational scheme of any school need to be in harmony.

Content versus Process

There persists an argument about the relative merits of what is called a content-centered approach to organization of culture content within a curriculum and a process-centered approach. For curriculum theorists, this appears to be an argument that warrants considerable attention. Something that adds to the confusion is that writers assign various meanings to the terms content and process, and the theorist is then confronted with the problem of selecting or establishing his own definition of such technical terms. Some of the meanings associated with these terms will illustrate the complexity of the problem.

The original dichotomization of the terms content and process probably occurred over arguments about whether teachers should be predominantly concerned with a body of content to be learned by pupils or with pupil learning processes. In actual fact, the answer never has been one or the other. The argument arose as a result of the shifting of emphasis from content to be learned to the learning processes — the latter an area that dominated professional effort during the 1920's and the 1930's and again in very recent years. A second distinction was made between the content of a subject and behavioral processes of applying elements of the content of the subject to the solution of social and practical problems. Here again, we can see that no real choice exists for the curriculum planner. There has been much discussion about the content of the disciplines and the modes of inquiry associated with them. We will highlight more of this argument in subsequent discussion of the disciplines and their structures as a basis for organizing the culture content within a curriculum.

An interesting position has been taken by Parker and Rubin that tends to dissolve the problem of content and process conceived as a dichotomy.[18] They contend that process should be interpreted as content in curriculum designing. They cite the following four tasks for the curriculum worker:

1. A retooling of subject matter to illuminate base structure, and to insure that knowledge which generates knowledge takes priority over knowledge which does not;
2. An examination of the working methods of the intellectual practitioner: the biologist, the historian, the political scientist, for the significant processes of their craft, and the use of these processes in our classroom instruction;
3. The utilization of the evidence gathered from a penetrating study of people doing things, as they go about the business of life, in reordering the curriculum;
4. A deliberate effort to school the child in the conditions for cross-application of the processes he has mastered — the ways and means of putting them to good use elsewhere.[19]

It is apparent that Parker and Rubin consider that the working methods of the intellectual practitioner in the disciplines is just as much a legitimate part of the culture content to be specified in a curriculum as are the generalizations or factual information with respect to the substance of the discipline in question. Certainly, information or skills that help an individual to make use of knowledge in any applied situation would similarly apply. Most of

---

[18]J. Cecil Parker and Lewis J. Rubin, *Process as Content: Curriculum Design and the Application of Knowledge* (Chicago: Rand McNally and Company, 1966).

[19]*Ibid.*, p. 48.

the discussion of the heuristics of curriculum content in recent years would fit or substantiate this argument.

Disciplines and Their Structures

Another task for the curriculum theorist as he seeks better explanations for the organization of culture content is to determine the nature of the disciplines and their structures and to assess their curriculum implications. There has been a plethora of publications advancing the proposition that curriculum content should be organized around the established disciplines. These publications have been reviewed again and again in such journals as the *Review of Educational Research* and in numerous books and pamphlets; thus, there is no need for a further review of them here. A number of references are cited at the end of this chapter for those who wish to delve into the details. Our exclusive purpose here is to assess the implications of the issue for curriculum design.

A discipline generally is thought to be a branch of knowledge that is organized so as to facilitate its instruction and its further development. It consists of a related series of concepts and principles which constitute the domain of the discipline. This is the culture content, or organized knowledge, generated by those who have worked in the discipline. A discipline has characteristic ways of behavior for the solution of problems. A discipline has a history, or a tradition, accumulated in the process of generating knowledge and developing unique ways of solving problems.

In his analysis of the structures of disciplines, Schwab identified three basic problem areas: the organization of a discipline, the substantive structures of a discipline, and the syntactical structures of a discipline.[20] The organization of a discipline refers to its orientation with respect to other disciplines. Orientation is helpful in curriculum organization in determining which discipline areas may be joined together and which need to remain separate. The substantive structures of a discipline refer to the knowledge produced by the discipline. For curriculum design, the substantive structures may be interpreted as those parts of the content needed to be understood by pupils. Syntactical structures

---

[20]Joseph J. Schwab, "Problems, Topics and Issues," *Education and the Structure of Knowledge*, ed. Stanley Elam (Chicago, Rand McNally and Company, 1964), pp. 4-43.

of a discipline refer to the modes and rules for generating proof or new knowledge. Ways in which scholars in the various disciplines gather and evaluate data, pose their hypotheses, and assert their generalizations are receiving a great deal of current attention as part of curriculum content.

The main thesis of those who have pushed for "discipline-centeredness" in curriculum design has been stated by Phenix in this way:

> . . .*all* curriculum content should be drawn from the disciplines, or, to put it another way, that *only* knowledge contained in the disciplines is appropriate to the curriculum.[21]

King and Brownell accept the same thesis as Phenix when they postulate that those who are qualified members of the discipline group of scholars should participate in curriculum planning.[22] They too would eliminate all nondiscipline knowledge from a curriculum.

The problem of sequence is solved by the selection of topics from the organized disciplines and the spiraling of them in terms of difficulty for various age groups. Bruner stated the hypothesis ". . . any subject can be taught effectively in some intellectually honest form to any child at any state of development."[23] He proposed a spiral curriculum graduated in difficulty from the simple to the complex. It is important to note that the criteria for selection, scope, and sequence as curriculum design features are all based upon the inherent worth of the knowledge and the modes of inquiry characteristic of the disciplines.

A special case of the application of discipline-centeredness to curriculum design is exhibited by those who are creating programmed materials for instruction. Two cases will illustrate, both in mathematics. One is the work carried on by Patrick Suppes at Stanford University on computerized instruction in mathematics. Suppes has developed carefully programmed sequences for the development of concepts and the ability to solve problems in which children must apply those concepts. The use of

---

[21]Philip H. Phenix, "The Disciplines as Curriculum Content," *Curriculum Crossroads*, ed. A. Harry Passow (New York: Bureau of Publications, Teachers College, Columbia University, 1962), p. 57.

[22]Arthur R. King, Jr. and John A. Brownell, *The Curriculum and the Disciplines of Knowledge* (New York: John Wiley and Sons, Inc., 1966).

[23]Jerome S. Bruner, *The Process of Education* (Cambridge: Harvard University Press, 1961), p. 33.

the computer in instruction provides for individualized instruction. The computer-based teaching machines provide immediate feedback and corrective measures when necessary. A second illustration is the University of Maryland mathematics project. In this program each learning step is programmed so that a hierarchical sequence of "learning sets" results. Positive transfer is assumed from one level to a higher level of learning sets. Exercises for pupils are provided, and appropriate achievement tests administered. Although the two examples cited were programmed sequences in mathematics, such carefully articulated programs are being worked out in virtually every discipline.

In addition to carefully worked out sequences spanning the structure of a discipline, there are prepared packages of materials, sometimes known as Learning Activity Packages (LAP's). LAP's have a carefully worked out structure that includes desired learning outcomes, varieties of media and resources for achieving objectives, and alternative means for completing the package. LAP's are different from the programs described in mathematics in several ways:

1. They assume that the users will be guided in their use of the package;

2. The outcomes are important and the users are free to deviate from the prescribed program or to choose from a variety of means to achieve the desired ends providing they can demonstrate that objectives have been satisfied;

3. They are generally planned for a topic and make no attempt to articulate objectives to span the structure of a discipline.

There are additional examples of prepared packages which are *not* discipline-centered. One such example is the social science program called *Man: A Course of Study*[24] (MACOS). MACOS attempts to provide a mesh of Bruner's instructional and Piaget's learning theories. That is, the learner structures his own knowledge in environments that offer multiple media and resource choices ranging from concrete to abstract and from simple to complex. The package itself focuses on man's humanity and seeks to explore the answers to the program's organizing

---

[24]Curriculum Development Associates, *Man: A Course of Study* (Cambridge: Education Development Center, Inc., 1969).

questions: (1) What makes man human? (2) How did he get that way? and (3) How can he be more so? Subject matter is drawn from several disciplines and from observations of social anthropologists doing field experiments. Using Bruner's idea of the spiral curriculum, animal behaviors that range from the most simple and dependent on the environment to the most complex and internalized are studied. Rather than drawing from any particular discipline, five humanizing forces, considered to be universal, provide the foci that help the learner to understand progressively more complex and internalized behavior. At the same time, they allow the learner to compare and contrast the behaviors at each succeedingly higher step.

There are two reasons for efforts like these to be considered as special cases in curriculum design. One is the careful programming of content. The other is that programs of this kind not only create curriculum answers to the question of what should be taught in schools; they also provide the instructional strategies and modes of appraisal. In this sense, they are unitary packages designed to solve the many problems of schooling.

Form and Arrangement

Any concept of curriculum design must account for the form and arrangement of the culture content. Under a discipline-centered, or a subject-centered, scheme, each of the subjects is arranged sequentially so that the various subtopics fit the vertical organization of the school; however, interrelationships among the chosen subjects, or disciplines, tend to be ignored. Bellack stated the problem as follows:

> When one looks beyond the structure of the individual disciplines and asks about the structure of the curriculum, attention is focused on *relationships* among the various fields that comprise the program of studies. For just as relationships among ideas is at the heart of the concept of structure as applied to the individual disciplines, so relationships among the disciplines is at the heart of the notion of structure as applied to the curriculum as a whole.[25]

At the heart of this problem is the quest for better explanations in

---

[25]Arno A. Bellack, "The Structure of Knowledge and the Structure of the Curriculum," *A Reassessment of the Curriculum*, ed. Dwayne Huebner (New York: Bureau of Publications, Teachers College, Columbia University, 1964), p. 28.

respect to the selection of culture content ingredients. Presumably, one selects culture content that will fulfill the goals set for education in schools. If it is possible to be convinced that the goals for schooling are achieved best by curriculum planners organizing the total culture content into discrete disciplines, or subjects, then it is reasonable to expect goal fulfillment to be directed by such design. On the other hand, if the goals set for schooling call for planned interrelationships among the various disciplines, or subjects, it is unreasonable to predict their achievement from a design composed of discretely organized components. Very few would argue that knowledge taken from disciplines and their structures is not important for the school curriculum, but many would take the position, as did Bellack, that curriculum design is more complicated. One of the more significant variations in design theory could be centered around positions taken with respect to intradisciplinary organization versus interdisciplinary organization.

The complex nature of educational goals makes the task of form and arrangement of culture content difficult. Goals may be classified into four categories: cognitive, syntactical, affective, and applicative. The first, cognitive, includes the basic concepts of knowledge, key ideas, generalizations, principles, and laws. It is in response to this goal category that school curriculums have provided content to be learned. The second, syntactical, consists of modes of inquiry for solving problems in the areas of organized knowledge such as observation, classification, inference, and prediction. It also includes the psychomotor skills of communication. The third consists of the development of affective behaviors. This is the domain of values, beliefs, emotions, attitudes, and appreciations. The fourth includes the development of abilities to make applications of learning to social and personal problems of living, particularly problems demanding that knowledge and skills developed in the first three categories be applied. A curriculum for today's schools must serve all of these. They have been talked about extensively, but little has been done to fulfill all of them. In part, the reason has been that traditional organization of culture content does not easily reveal relationships between the identified goals and the culture content. This may be one of the reasons why the statement of our educational goals in the form of specific behavioral objectives has become popular. A specific objective is easy to relate to any one of the four categories indicated above. In any event, the organization of culture content that may lead to the achievement of our various types of goals is a challenging task for those who address themselves to the problems of curriculum design.

We should keep in mind that what we are talking about at this moment is the form and arrangement of the culture content, or subject matter, that may be a part of the total contents of a curriculum. The portion of the curriculum having to do with the organization of the culture content is more closely related to the instructional strategies that teachers make in response to a curriculum than any other section. It therefore is extremely important. However, it is the form and arrangement of the culture content that has been most often discussed under curriculum design or patterns of curriculum organization. We have discussed some of the historical arrangements, and now we need to look at possibilities for the form and arrangement of the total contents of a curriculum.

Ralph Tyler has long been concerned with curriculum organization. Tyler identified as organizing elements for a curriculum the concepts, skills, and values cited as behavioral objectives for pupils. Specific subjects, broad fields, core lessons, topics, or units he referred to as organizing structures. Organizing principles called for use of chronological order, extension outward from pupils' lives, the use of concrete materials and ideas prior to abstraction, and increasing the breadth and application of knowledge.[26]

Another type of design for the culture content of a curriculum is that conceived and advocated by Stratemeyer, *et al.*[27] This particular design is based upon the concept of persistent life situations. Persistent life situations are defined as "those situations that recur in the life of the individual in many different ways as he grows from infancy to maturity."[28] The major areas within which

---

[26]Ralph W. Tyler, "Curriculum Organization," *The Integration of Educational Experiences*, Fifty-seventh Yearbook, National Society for the Study of Education, Part III (Chicago: The University of Chicago Press, 1958), pp. 105-125.

[27]Florence B. Stratemeyer, Hamden L. Forkner, Margaret G. McKim, and A. Harry Passow, *Developing A Curriculum for Modern Living* (2d ed.; New York: Bureau of Publications, Teachers College, Columbia University, 1957).

[28]*Ibid.*, p. 45.

persistent life situations are found are health, intellectual power, moral choices, aesthetic expression and appreciation, person-to-person relationships, group membership, intergroup relationships, natural phenomena, technological resources, and economic-social-political structures and forces. Within each of the major areas, specific persistent life situations are identified. For example, under the major area "intellectual power," Stratemeyer includes making oral presentations, expressing ideas in written form, using graphic forms to express ideas, using source materials, understanding symbols and relationships, budgeting time and energy, and solving practical problems that persistently recur.[29] Individuals face situations like these in more or less complicated form depending upon their level of growth and maturity; thus curriculum design must account for them. The reader will observe that a design of the persistent life situations type is drastically different from a design that employs disciplines and their structures as a fundamental point of departure. The same may be said of core, broad fields, or social problems as basic orientations. The discipline-centered approach proceeds from the logical organization of selected portions of the disciplines which themselves are logically organized. The persistent life situations type proceeds from perceived social, cultural, and personal needs of the school pupils. In this sense, it is psychologically oriented.

Another proposal for the form and arrangement of culture content is that elaborated by Broudy, Smith, and Burnett.[30] It should be noted first that Broudy, Smith, and Burnett believe that the secondary school should be an institution to provide for the general education of the adolescent population. They reject the notion of terminal, or vocational education, as the responsibility of the secondary school. The pros and cons of this argument obviously cannot be given here in detail, but the point is essential to an understanding of the design proposal. For Broudy, Smith, and Burnett, curriculum consists primarily of two elements. One of the elements is content which is characterized by facts, descriptive and valuative concepts, principles, and norms and rules. The other element consists of categories of instruction organized under

---

[29]*Ibid.*, pp. 155-165.

[30]Harry S. Broudy, B. Othanel Smith, and Joe R. Burnett, *Democracy and Excellence in American Secondary Education* (Chicago: Rand McNally and Company, 1964).

symbolic studies, basic sciences, developmental studies, aesthetic studies, and molar problems.[31] The specific design features of this proposal are illustrated in Figure 7. Certainly, this design is radically different from the usual array of required and elective courses that is traditional with our secondary schools.

In the 1966 Goodlad and Richter monograph previously quoted, the authors proposed a conceptual system for dealing with problems of curriculum and instruction.[32] Since they were primarily concerned with setting forth a rationale for dealing with problems of curriculum, one has to infer from their discussion what characteristics might be present in curriculum design. Figure 8 portrays that portion of the Goodlad and Richter rationale that has greatest implications for curriculum design. For Goodlad and Richter all educational aims stem from the accepted cultural values. Educational aims would be translated into educational objectives stated behaviorally. These in turn would lead to learning opportunities. The authors define a learning opportunity as "a situation created within the context of an educational program or institution for the purpose of achieving certain educational ends."[33] Specification of courses or categories of readings and writing are examples of learning opportunities. Both the general educational objectives and the learning opportunities would be identifiable in two categories, one of the categories having a behavioral element and the other category having a substantive element. From the selected learning opportunities and from the general educational objectives, more specific educational objectives stated behaviorally are formulated; these, in turn, lead to the selection of organizing centers. An organizing center is defined as "a specific learning opportunity set up for identifiable students or for a student."[34] Field trips, problems, or topics are examples of organizing centers.

Drawing heavily upon the notions of behavioral elements and substantive elements in curriculum design, Dellard surveyed proposals for curriculum design published between 1960 and 1972, and developed a conceptual scheme by which various design

---

[31]*Ibid.* p. 83.
[32]*Op. cit.*
[33]*Ibid.*, p. 18.
[34]*Ibid.*, p. 18.

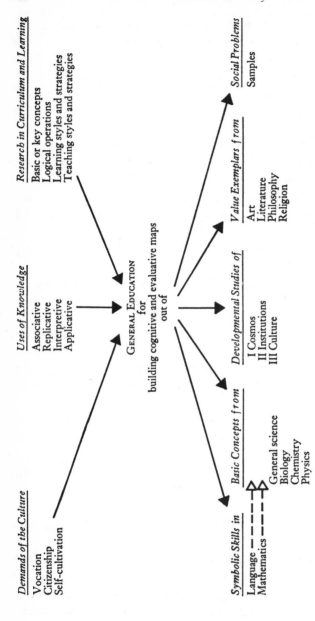

Figure 7. *Design for common curriculum in general education (grades 7-12).* Adapted by permission from Harry S. Broudy, B. Othanel Smith, and Joe R. Burnett, *Democracy and Excellence in American Secondary Education* (Chicago: Rand McNally and Company, 1964), p. 160.

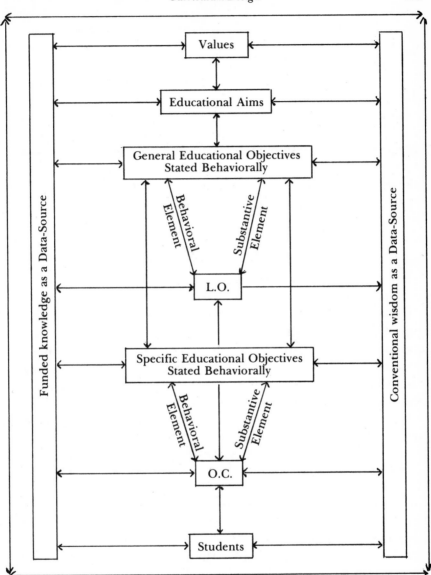

Figure 8. *Substantive decisions and derivations in a conceptual system for curriculum.* Adapted by permission from John I. Goodlad and Maurice N. Richter, Jr., *The Development of A Conceptual System for Dealing with Problems of Curriculum and Instruction* (Los Angeles: Institute for Development of Educational Activities, University of California, 1966, p. 65.

proposals could be systematically categorized and analyzed.[35] She was led to classify curriculum design proposals into three categories: (1) one-dimensional substantive designs, (2) one-dimensional behavioral designs, (3) two-dimensional designs. To be classified as one-dimensional substantive, a design had to rest upon such information as subjects, concepts, ideas, facts, or generalizations. Similarly, to qualify as a one-dimensional behavioral design, a design had to be based upon such behaviors as processes, attitudes, values, and so forth. Two-dimensional designs contained both substantive and behavioral material with an identified relationship or integration between the two classes of materials.

TRENDS IN PRACTICE

What goes on in practice is a convenient way for anyone to analyze curriculum design characteristics. One may review the contents of curriculums or of curriculum guides. Merritt and Harap did a thorough job of this in 1955.[36] They surveyed published courses of study and analyzed the content of those materials in detail. The authors found some new trends, especially in the production of guides for the subject areas of art, business education, and kindergarten. More to the point here, they also discerned a pattern in the contents of the guides surveyed. More than one-half of them contained general objectives as goals to be attained in a specific subject area while one-third contained general objectives stated as outcomes. The finding which startled the authors was the omission of basic views and policies affecting the teaching of the subject for the course. This omission was an indication to the investigators that too many guides were mere outlines of content to be learned. The infrequent inclusion of such considerations as scope, sequence, the nature of the unit of the work, and others, supported their conclusion.

Much later a similar study was conducted by Langenbach and others.[37] In that study, 1002 documents from school systems were

---

[35]Cynthia Dellard, "A Systematic Survey of Curriculum Design Proposals from 1960 to 1972 " (A Master's Paper, Northwestern University, July, 1972).

[36]Eleanor Merritt and Henry Harap, *Trends in the Production of Curriculum Guides* (Nashville: Division of Surveys and Field Services, George Peabody College for Teachers, 1955).

[37]Michael Langenbach, Michael T. Hinkemeyer, and George A. Beauchamp, "An Empirical Analysis of Curriculum Design," *Research in Education*, ED045 582, 6:146, April, 1971.

examined. The documents were purported to be curriculum materials, and they were included in the "Curriculum Materials Exhibit" at the 1969 national conference of the Association for Supervision and Curriculum Development, N.E.A. The materials were submitted voluntarily. They came from all sections of the country, and they were of recent origin. The analysis of the design features of those documents presented a picture of what curriculums planned in school districts and individual schools do look like. The documents were subject-centered in design. A classification of the materials into major types gave the following results:

Type	*Number*
General Curriculum	69
Art	29
Business Education	20
Foreign Language	21
Health, Physical Education, and Safety	77
Home Economics	21
Industrial and Vocational Education	74
Language Arts	195
Mathematics	97
Music	40
Science	113
Social Studies	246
TOTAL	1002

It can be seen from the above distribution that most of the curriculum documents were on individual school subjects and that sixty-nine of them were classified as general curriculums; that is, they covered more than one subject and for more than one grade. Most of the individual subject documents were designed for a school level such as the elementary or the secondary school.

More than 65 per cent of the documents included objectives, subject outlines, instructional materials, and pupil activities. Approximately one-fourth of them were topically organized within a subject, and one-half of them were organized on a unit basis. Ninety-five per cent contained statements of goals or objectives; of these, more than 50 per cent were stated in behavioral terms.

Several other kinds of entries add to the total design picture of the materials. More than 60 per cent of them contained historical statements about the development of the material. Eighty-four per cent gave instructions that the materials were to be used by teachers to develop their teaching strategies; yet 73 per cent of the documents contained statements that could be interpreted as being instructional strategies. Only 15 per cent contained any kind of evaluation scheme.

From the foregoing descriptive statements about curriculum materials produced at the level of school practice, several conclusions may be reached. The basic design pattern was subject-centered, and the vast majority of the documents were devoted to a single subject. Planners appeared to consider it important to include in curriculums: objectives, subject outlines, instructional materials, and pupil activities.

Most curriculums, or curriculum guides, or curriculum materials include what may be termed instructional guides; that is they contain various kinds of directions for teachers pertaining to methods. And for the most part, they are organized by subject. In them, more instructions are given customarily to teachers in elementary curriculums than in secondary ones. This seems to constitute a vote of greater faith in the instructional ingenuity of the secondary school teacher than of the elementary teacher. Irrespective of this issue, there is great variation in the size of instructional guides as indicated by the number of pages devoted to a subject as well as by the content on the pages. There is a trend toward detailing the entries so as to solve instructional problems. The trend is reflected in the amount of attention given to instructional materials and teaching strategies. More of this kind of detail is present when instructional guides are published by subject rather than as general guides. Curriculum offices in large city school systems tend to prepare larger volumes than the smaller school districts.

Rarely do curriculums contain evaluation schemes or specific implementation instructions. The former probably reflects our artlessness about evaluation in general and about curriculum in particular. Lack of specific implementation instructions may mean that they are provided by some means such as administrative dictum. It may be a reflection of fear of imposing too rigidly upon the rights of teachers to decide their own teaching strategies.

SUMMARY AND A POINT OF VIEW

More controversy exists within the field of curriculum over issues in curriculum design than anything else. To attempt a thorough summary of all the issues would be to repeat most of what has been said previously in this chapter. By way of summary, therefore, I shall merely indicate which aspects of curriculum design spawn most of the issues, and then spend the rest of this section briefly outlining what my own point of view is with respect to curriculum design.

Summary

Most issues in curriculum design originate with one's conception of what a curriculum is, and this conception is usually reflected in a definition of a curriculum. As has been indicated in the earlier paragraphs, curriculum design is drastically different for the individual who defines a curriculum as a set of intended learning outcomes as compared with a person who defines a curriculum as all of the experiences that students have in school. Conceptually, these two definitions are worlds apart. If they may be considered as extremes in points of view, lesser differences appear for those who conceptualize a curriculum differently from these two.

People differ over whether a curriculum should be a written document or not. Most other issues with respect to curriculum design are dissolved if one accepts the notion that a curriculum is not a written document; therefore, any subsequent issues with respect to curriculum design are dependent upon the assumption that a curriculum is a written document. With these assumptions in mind we can review issues pertaining to document features or the content of a curriculum. Document features are simplified if one believes that a curriculum is only a set of statements of expected learning outcomes or behavioral objectives. Specific outcomes would normally be identified within some framework such as the subjects to be offered in school. On the other hand, if one also expects there to be included in a curriculum a body of culture content that is selected in anticipation that the culture content will assist in the achievement of the goals or objectives, then ways must be sought for organizing that culture content. It is at this point that we have a very real theoretical issue between contemporary curriculum theorists. The issue simply is whether the selection of culture content shall be done at the level of instructional planning or at the level of curriculum planning.

Historically, there have been many issues created over the character of the culture content to be included in the curriculum. Again, the argument has been whether the culture content should be organized logically or psychologically. This may be interpreted as subject-centered versus experience-centered organization of culture content. In recent years, the issue has mostly been focused upon substantive culture content and processes of learning.

A third category of issue is whether to include instructional materials in a curriculum as well as the degree of their specificity. When these materials are incorporated into a curriculum, they usually include such things as suggested instructional materials and student activities. This issue reverts to definition again. It is only an issue when the curriculum position, or theory, incorporates curriculum planning and the planning of instructional strategies as part of curriculum designing. Many persons who write curriculum books apparently fall into the latter category, but those who write extensively about curriculum theory tend not to.

What else might be included in a curriculum beyond those mentioned above is discussed by very few people. I am one of the few who do, as I will illustrate in the following and concluding section of this chapter.

A Point of View

To illustrate how a theorist might select from the issues that have been summarized above in order to establish a consistent position with respect to curriculum design, I shall use my own position. The essential dimensions of my position on curriculum design are reflected in the model shown in Figure 9.

For me, a curriculum minimally has three properties or characteristics: (1) it is a written document; (2) it contains statements outlining the goals for the school for which the curriculum was designed; and (3) it contains a body of culture content that tentatively has the potential for the realization of the

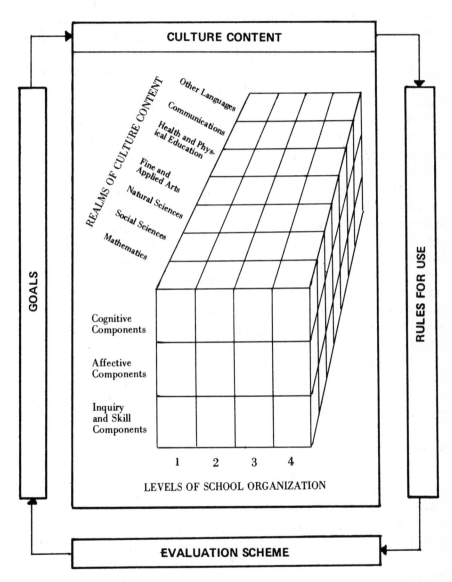

Figure 9. *A model for curriculum design.*

goals. Optimally, I would add two to those: a statement of intention for use of the document as a guiding force for planning instructional strategies and an evaluation scheme. It seems to me that it is axiomatic that anyone who talks about a curriculum needs first to conceive of it as a written document. It is quite improbable that anything other than a written document reflecting curriculum thinking could have organized design characteristics. Thus by definition, a curriculum is a written plan depicting the scope and arrangement of the projected educational program for a school.

In Figure 9, provision is made for a statement of goals, or purposes for the school. At the level of curriculum planning, it appears to me that it would be more realistic to phrase these goal statements in general terms and leave the preparation of highly specific behavioral objectives to the level of instructional planning. In the model under discussion, a large part of a curriculum would consist of the culture content organization. Culture content is designated in terms of language, communications, health and physical education, fine and applied arts, natural sciences, social sciences, mathematics, and molar problems. One might substitute for the foregoing designations the patterns of meanings used by Phenix,[38] namely, symbolics, empirics, aesthetics, synnoetics, ethics, and synoptics. Or, one might substitute the categories of instruction listed by Broudy, Smith, and Burnett: symbolic studies, basic sciences, developmental studies, aesthetic studies, and molar problems. I would have no objection to either substitution. I have chosen the ones included in Figure 9 because I believe that most curriculum planners would feel more comfortable with the designations I have used. In this connection, anyone who must make this choice will do so on the basis of some established belief because there simply is no research literature demonstrating that one produces better results than the other. In Figure 9, the culture content is also identified in terms of characteristics of the culture content other than the designations listed above. These are called cognitive components, affective components, and inquiry and skill components. These characteristic components are included so that the culture content may be more specifically related to goals, and so that the

---

[38]*Op. cit.*

curriculum will project a better level of advice for teachers who are to subsequently use the curriculum for developing instructional strategies. Across the bottom of the chart four levels of school organization are indicated. Normally, these would be labeled in terms of the actual administrative organization of the school as grades, levels, or ordinal years. This three-way organization of the culture content would force curriculum planners to be concerned with such design characteristics as scope, sequence, and vertical and horizontal articulation.

Two additional ingredients are included in the design model. One is a set of rules or statements designating how the curriculum is to be used and how it is to be modified as a result of experience in using the curriculum. These rules are extremely important in order to keep the curriculum constantly under scrutiny and revised in accordance with the best thinking of the planners. The final ingredient indicated on the right hand side of the model is an evaluation scheme. The evaluation scheme should at least outline the ways in which the curriculum is to be evaluated with respect to its design features as well as evaluation of the system of curriculum engineering of which is the subject matter of the subsequent chapter.

SUGGESTED READINGS

Alberty, Harold B. and Elsie J. Alberty. *Reorganizing the High-School Curriculum.* 3d ed. New York: The Macmillan Company, 1962.

Alexander, William M. *Changing Curriculum Content: Report of the Conference on Curriculum Content.* Washington: Association for Supervision and Curriculum Development, NEA, 1964.

Alpren, Morton (ed.). *The Subject Curriculum: Grades K-12.* Columbus, Ohio: Charles E. Merrill Books, Inc., 1967.

Ammons, Margaret. "The Definition, Function, and Use of Educational Objectives," *The Elementary School Journal,* 62:432-436, May, 1962.

Ammons, Margaret and Robert S. Gilchrist. *Assessing and Using Curriculum Content.* Washington, D.C.: Association for Supervision and Curriculum Development, NEA, 1965.

Anderson, Dan W., James B. Macdonald, and Frank B. May (eds.). *Strategies of Curriculum Development.* Columbus: Charles E. Merrill Books, Inc., 1965.

Beauchamp, George A. *The Curriculum of the Elementary School.* Boston: Allyn and Bacon, Inc., 1964.

Beckner, Weldon, and Joe D. Cornett. *The Secondary School Curriculum: Content and Structure.* Scranton, Pa.: Intext Educational Publishers, 1972.

Bloom, Benjamin S. (ed.). *Taxonomy of Educational Objectives: Handbook I Cognitive Domain.* New York: Longmans, Green and Company, 1956.

Broudy, Harry S., B. Othanel Smith and Joe R. Burnett. *Democracy and Excellence in American Secondary Education.* Chicago: Rand McNally and Company, 1964.

Bruner, Jerome S. *The Process of Education.* Cambridge: Harvard University Press, 1961.

Educational Policies Commission. *The Central Purpose of American Education.* Washington: the Commission, 1961.

Elam, Stanley (ed.). *Education and the Structure of Knowledge.* Chicago: Rand McNally and Company, 1964.

Firth, Gerald R. and Richard D. Kimpston. *The Curricular Continuum in Perspective.* Itasca, Ill.: F.E. Peacock Publishers, Inc., 1973.

Ford, G. W. and Lawrence Pugno (eds.). *The Structure of Knowledge and the Curriculum.* Chicago: Rand McNally and Company, 1964.

Foshay, Arthur W. "A Modest Proposal," *Educational Leadership,* 18:506-516, May, 1961.

Frost, J. L. and G. T. Rowland. *Curricula for the Seventies.* New York: Houghton-Mifflin Company, 1969.

Goodlad, John I., and Maurice N. Richter, Jr. *The Development of a Conceptual System for Dealing with Problems of Curriculum and Instruction.* Los Angeles: Institute for Development of Educational Activities, University of California, 1966. (ERIC ED010064)

Heath, Robert W. (ed.). *New Curricula.* New York: Harper and Row, 1964.

Huebner, Dwayne (ed.). *A Reassessment of the Curriculum.* New York: Bureau of Publications, Teachers College, Columbia University, 1964.

Hughes, Philip. "Decisions and Curriculum Design," *Educational Theory,* 12:187-192, July, 1962.

Inlow, Gail M. *The Emergent in Curriculum.* 2d ed. New York: John Wiley and Sons, Inc., 1973.

Johnson, Mauritz, Jr. "Definitions and Models in Curriculum Theory," *Educational Theory,* 17:127-140, April, 1967.

Kearney, Nolan C. *Elementary School Objectives: A Report Prepared for the Mid-Century Committee on Outcomes in Elementary Education.* New York: Russell Sage Foundation, 1953.

King, Arthur R. and John A. Brownell. *The Curriculum and the Disciplines of Knowledge.* New York: John Wiley and Sons, Inc., 1966.

Krathwohl, David R., Benjamin S. Bloom, and Bertram B. Masia. *Taxonomy of Educational Objectives: Handbook II Affective Domain.* New York: David McKay Company, Inc., 1964.

Krug, Edward A. *Curriculum Planning.* Rev. ed. New York: Harper and Row, 1957.

Merritt, Eleanor and Henry Harap. *Trends in the Production of Curriculum Guides.* Nashville: Division of Surveys and Field Service, George Peabody College for Teachers, 1955.

Michaelis, John V., Ruth H. Grossman, and Lloyd F. Scott. *New Designs for the Elementary School Curriculum.* New York: McGraw-Hill Book Company, 1967.

Parker, J. Cecil and Louis J. Rubin. *Process as Content: Curriculum Design and the Application of Knowledge.* Chicago: Rand McNally and Company, 1966.

Passow, A. Harry (ed.). *Curriculum Crossroads.* New York: Bureau of Publications, Teachers College, Columbia University, 1962.

Phenix, Philip H. *Realms of Meaning.* New York: McGraw-Hill Book Company, 1964.

Ragan, William B. and G. D. Shepherd. *Modern Elementary Curriculum.* 4th ed. New York: Holt, Rinehart and Winston, Inc., 1971.

Saylor, J. Galen and William M. Alexander. *Planning Curriculum for Schools.* New York: Holt, Rinehart, and Winston, Inc., 1974.

Smith, B. Othanel, William O. Stanley, and J. Harlan Shores. *Fundamentals of Curriculum Development.* Rev. ed. Yonkers-on-Hudson: World Book Company, 1957.

Stratemeyer, Florence B., Hamden L. Forkner, Margaret C. McKim, and A. Harry Passow. *Developing a Curriculum for Modern Living.* 2d ed. New York: Bureau of Publication, Teachers College, Columbia University, 1957.

Taba, Hilda. *Curriculum Development: Theory and Practice.* New York: Harcourt, Brace and World, Inc., 1962.

Taylor, Philip H. *Purpose and Structure in the Curriculum.* An Inaugural Lecture delivered in the University of Birmingham, England on November 3, 1966.

Tyler, Ralph W. "Curriculum Organization," *The Integration of Educational Experiences.* Fifty-seventh Yearbook of the National Society for the Study of Education, Part III, 1958, pp. 105-125.

Unruh, Glenys G. (ed.). *New Curriculum Developments.* Washington: Association for Supervision and Curriculum Development, NEA., 1965.

Chapter 7

CURRICULUM ENGINEERING

The phrase "Curriculum Engineering" as title for this chapter demands explanation. A large portion of curriculum literature has dealt with the problems with curriculum planning, development, or improvement, thus, focusing upon the production of curriculums or curriculum materials. Only a small portion of the literature has reflected thinking about curriculum implementation, and until recently, the subject of curriculum evaluation has largely been ignored. The processes of planning, implementing, and evaluating a curriculum may be spoken of as the essential processes of a curriculum system. A curriculum system is a system for both decision making and action with respect to curriculum functions regarded as a part of the total operations of schooling. As indicated, the system has three primary functions: (1) to produce a curriculum, (2) to implement the curriculum, and (3) to appraise the effectiveness of the curriculum and the curriculum system. The primary ingredient in effectuating these functions is decision making by the persons involved, and the decision-making tasks are complicated both by the nature of the tasks and the number of persons involved. The complications call for intelligent human engineering if the functions are to be carried out effectively. Hence, the title of curriculum engineering is used to represent both the system and its internal dynamics.

Curriculum engineering consists of all of the processes necessary to make a curriculum system functional in schools. The chief engineers in the curriculum system are the superintendent of schools, principals, and curriculum directors, and they may be assisted by consultative personnel from outside the school system.

They, the engineers, organize and direct the manipulation of the various tasks and operations that must go on in order for a curriculum to be planned, implemented in classrooms through the instructional program, evaluated, and revised in light of the data accumulated through evaluation. Thus, curriculum engineering encompasses the set of activities necessary to keep the curriculum of a school in a dynamic state.

In this chapter, the scope of curriculum engineering activities will be identified by pointing up the critical areas of concern in any curriculum system and by noting how alternative choices would be related to different theoretical positions. Before turning to these critical choices, it is necessary for us to describe more carefully than we have done so far the precise character of the more important systems of schooling, and the characteristics of a curriculum system.

SYSTEMS OF SCHOOLING

A convenient way for theorists and practitioners to identify a curriculum system and its prescribed roles is to observe its place among other systems of schooling. By schooling is meant all those activities essential to the purposeful maintenance and operation of schools. The systems of schooling are operational constructs that explain the character of schooling, and that have identifiable internal characteristics. These can be represented diagrammatically, one such diagram being included here as Figure 10. In it, the language of set relationships is used to explain the interrelationships among the various systems of schooling. The symbol U designates the universal set, or universe of discourse, which represents schooling. Subset A represents the curriculum system. Subset B represents the instructional system, and subset C represents the evaluation system. The remaining space within U represents all subsets, or systems, of schooling not included in A, B, and C. These might be the administrative system, the personnel services system, the guidance system and so forth. Our major concern here is with the three systems curriculum, instruction, and evaluation because they more nearly characterize the fundamental nature of schooling than any others.

The set intersections shown in Figure 10 are very interesting.

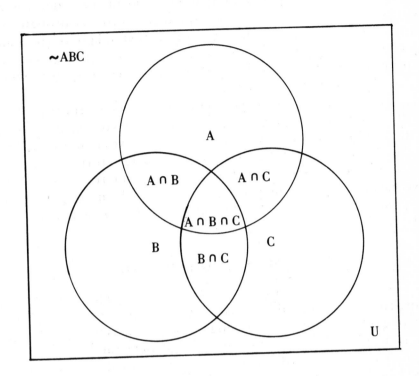

Legend:

U	=	the universe of discourse (the systems of schooling)
~ABC	=	all systems of schooling except systems A, B, and C
A	=	the curriculum system
B	=	the instruction system
C	=	the evaluation system
A ∩ B	=	the intersection of system A and system B
B ∩ C	=	the intersection of system B and system C
A ∩ C	=	the intersection of system A and system C
A ∩ B ∩ C	=	the intersection of system A, system B, and system C

Figure 10. *A diagram representing the systems of schooling.*

They represent the interactions of two or more of the three systems. This interaction, or overlay, of the systems graphically portrays the continuity among curriculum, instruction, and evaluation. It helps to establish that there are no discrete boundaries among systems, and that systems have purposes in common. For example, the intersection of curriculum and instruction might represent such functions as planning for implementation, lesson planning, and teacher-pupil planning. These functions bridge the gap between decisions about what to teach and decisions about how to teach. The intersection of curriculum and evaluation might represent the evaluation of the degree of curriculum implementation, evaluation of teacher use of the curriculum, evaluation of curriculum organization, or feedback of information from evaluation for curriculum revision. These functions bridge the gap between the decisions made about what to teach and the judgments made about the predictability and the worth of those decisions. The intersection of instruction and evaluation represents the functions that bridge the gap between activities associated with the execution of decisions about how to teach and appraisal of those activities via such means as diagnostic testing by the teacher, pupil self-evaluations, appraisal of teaching performances, or the evaluation of instructional materials. The intersection of all three systems is the payoff area of schooling. This intersection represents those pupil learnings intended by the curriculum system, sought through the instructional system, and observed in the evaluation system. All systems point toward pupil learnings. All systems make some contribution to pupil learnings. We can amplify distinctions among the three systems indicated in Figure 10 by indicating some of the characteristics of each in greater detail.

The Curriculum System

The general purpose of a curriculum system as one of the several systems of schooling is to provide a framework for deciding what ought to be taught in the schools and for employing those decisions as points of departure for developing instructional strategies. Every school and/or school district does some planning for schooling, carries out instruction, and appraises outcomes.

However, in many schools and districts, organization for curriculum decisions is invisible rather than visible, unconscious rather than conscious, and random rather than rational. When this condition prevails, we cannot say that a curriculum system is present. But when a deliberate and constant organization is used to plan the curriculum, implement it, and appraise its effectiveness, we may say that a curriculum system is present.

The language of systems analysis is useful in describing the basic characteristics of a curriculum system. Figure 11 is a diagram of a model of a curriculum system using that language. The system is composed of three essential components: (1) a body of input data, (2) the necessary content and processes for the maintenance of the system, and (3) the output of the system. In Figure 11, the entries under each of the three components are brief and generalized to avoid contamination by any specific position with respect to curriculum engineering. The purpose here is to illustrate what a system is and how it works regardless of specific choices any individual or group might make within the general system framework. We will return to specific choices with respect to the curriculum processes later in this discussion.

Input data. The function of input data is to provide energy for the content and processes that maintain the steady state of the system. Energy in this case is the intellectual and personal driving power engendered by such forces as educational foundations, relevant community characteristics, human personalities involved, experience of schools with curriculum affairs, the large body of human knowledge stored and categorized in the disciplines and other school subjects, and relevant social and cultural values. Many other specific classes of input data could be added to the list shown in Figure 11 such as commercial materials, projections from research, technological feasibility data, and identified needs and interests of learners, to mention just a few. Input data constitutes sources of authority, sources of new ideas, and general ways of behaving in carrying out the curriculum functions. Curriculum functions are carried out at the level of system maintenance. During the system maintenance processes, relevant information, procedures, and values have to be selected from the input sources. This selection process is one of the reasons why working in a full curriculum system is educative for the participants.

Input	Content and Processes for System Maintenance	Output

Educational foundations
Community characteristics
Personalities of persons involved
Curriculum experience
The subject matters from disciplines and other subjects
Social and cultural values
	Choice of arena for curriculum processes
	Selection of personnel
	Selection and execution of working procedures for:
	  determining curricular goals
	  selection of curriculum design
	  planning and writing
	Establishing implementation procedures
	Establishing procedures for appraising and revising the curriculum
		A curriculum
		Increased knowledge by participants
		Changed attitudes
		Commitment to act

Figure 11. *A model of a curriculum system.*

Content and processes for system maintenance. Any system is characterized by a known body of activities that make the system work and maintain itself. Figure 11 lists the basic functions that must go on for a curriculum system to be maintained. We shall mention them only briefly here because they are the areas of substantial issue and controversy in curriculum. The principal choices among them will be discussed in detail later. There is sequential order to the way these functions are listed in Figure 11. A first choice that must be made by those in authority for schooling is the arena in which curriculum activities are to take place. The arena is where curriculum planning is to be done and where implementation functions are to be directed. Once the arena choice has been made, the persons who are to be involved in curriculum decision making may be chosen. Once the persons to be involved have been identified, working procedures may be planned to determine the curricular goals, to select a curriculum design, to develop details of the design, and to write the curriculum. Procedures will have to be planned to move from the curriculum system to the instructional system; these constitute the implementation plans. Finally, plans need to be made to appraise the output of the curriculum system and the data used to revise both curriculum and the activities of the curriculum system. All of these are warranted ingredients of what may be called a curriculum system.

Output. The most obvious and necessary output of a curriculum system is a planned curriculum, and is the major visible output. Other outputs such as changed attitudes of teachers and other participants in the system, increased knowledge by the participants because the planning process has been educative, and a commitment by teachers and school leaders to implement and to appraise the curriculum are just as real as the planned curriculum, but they are not immediately visible.

Schools have a long history of curriculum planning, but not many have examined the outputs of those efforts. Even more important, curriculum practitioners have had little experience in using the results of examining curriculum outputs as feedback data to improve further curriculum efforts. To appraise the magnitude of these outputs, measures that will identify the traits involved and the magnitude of them will have to be constructed. The development of instruments that would give us these measures needs to be among the next steps of curriculum research.

Conran has made a substantial effort in this direction by studying the relationship among several variables in a curriculum engineering system in such a way that the effects of various performers in the curriculum system were identified.[1] The degree of relationship was determined among such variables as principal leadership, teacher attitudes, teacher experience and training, teacher performance, student sex and intelligence quotient, and student achievement. Still, more precise measurement of variables needs to be accomplished, more representative ways of modeling relationships need to be explored, and further study of additional relationships that would observe the effects of such variables as school climate and student motivation, among others, needs to be undertaken.

The Instructional System

To indicate differences and relationships among the input data, the system maintenance content and processes, and outputs for an instructional system as contrasted with a curriculum system, Figure 12 is included. It should be noted that the curriculum which was the principal output of the curriculum system is a principal input to the instructional system. Other inputs also vary according to the character of the system. It is most important, however, to note the differences between the content and processes for system maintenance included in the instructional system as compared with those in the curriculum system. This comparison virtually spells out in rather concrete terms the environmental and functional differences between the instructional system and the curriculum system. The primary output of the operation of the instructional system should be pupil learnings.

The Appraisal System

Some examples of what an appraisal system would be like are shown in Figure 13. The appraisal system is designed to provide a

---

[1]Patricia C. Conran, "A Study of Causal and Other Relationships among Leadership, Teacher, and Student Variables in Curriculum Engineering" (unpublished Doctoral dissertation, Northwestern University, 1974).

Input

The curriculum
Teacher characteristics
Pupil characteristics
Community resources
Available instructional
  materials
Building facilities
Financial resources
Library resources
Leadership

Content and Processes for System Maintenance

Development of teaching strategies including specific behavior of outcomes
Development of pupil-teacher strategies
Selection of instructional materials,
  and devices, and other resources
Organization of pupils
Execution of strategies through such
  activities as individual study, group
  investigation, discussion, projects,
  reports, programed learning, excur-
  sions, etc.
Use of appraisal strategies such as
  testing, observing, recording
Use of appraisal strategies such as
  testing,,observing, recording
  anecdotes, case studies, conferring,
  etc.
Teacher appraisal (by self and others)

Output

Pupil learnings
Identified need for
  curriculum change
Identified need for
  change in instruc-
  tional practices
Data for interpreta-
  tion

Figure 12. *A model of an instructional system.*

Input	Content and Processes for System Maintenance	Output
The curriculum	Achievement testing	Data for curriculum change
Data from instructional system	Anecdotal record system	Data for improvement of instruction
Known techniques	Collection of data on curriculum implementation	Data for social interpretation
Established pupil progress reporting procedures	Collection of data on needed curriculum change	
Available research skill	Collection of data on teacher proficiency	
Commercial testing materials	Reporting of pupil progress	
	Research on specific problems	
	Interpretation of schooling operations	

Figure 13. *A model of an appraisal system.*

trunk line of feedback data for the products and processes of the curriculum system and the instructional system. To be sure, the appraisal system would also similarly serve any other system such as the administrative system or the pupil-services system, but those are not of our primary concern here. Again, one should note particularly in the systems maintenance content and processes, a distinctly different group of functions than those listed in either the curriculum or the instructional system. Inputs to the system come from both the curriculum system and the instructional system as well as techniques and knowledge peculiar to the processes of evaluation. Outputs immediately lead back to the curriculum system and the instructional system thus providing a dynamic cycle of feedback and correction to the fundamental processes of schooling.

Conran's study of relationships among variables in a curriculum engineering system is an initial attempt to provide some of the intended feedback. She used mathematics in the form of reduced-form structural equations and the technique of path analysis to determine the strength of assumed relationships and to model relationships. Differences were observed among principals in leadership effectiveness; differences were noted between the ways principals rated teachers' performances compared with the way teachers perceived their own performances; and relationships among principal, teacher, and student variables were observed. This kind of information and future analyses of perhaps a more complex and precise nature can begin to give school personnel the kind of feedback necessary for planning individualized in-service programs, for improving employment practices, and for clarifying and revising policies and practices in the curriculum and the instructional systems.

Theoretical Issues

No doubt it is apparent to the reader that a grossly different theoretical position would be taken by an individual in the field of curriculum who would accept the notion that a curriculum system and an instructional system are all one. Nonetheless, the illustration of the two systems in terms of their content and processes for system maintenance do illustrate the total complexity of involving both systems in one's thinking about curriculum. Regardless of posture taken, the curriculum theorist finds more immediate food for his efforts in systems of curriculum engineering than in any other area of the total field of curriculum. The most plausible reason for this is the vast experience we have had in this country with curriculum planning. It is true that our experience with the task and method variables of curriculum implementation and curriculum evaluation has been limited; the reason is that we have not worked hard at these dimensions. But we have worked hard at the tasks and methods of curriculum planning. The alternative ways of accomplishing the various tasks of curriculum engineering provide the theorist with a basic classification scheme from which the beginning elements of curriculum theories may be deduced, and from which further research may be launched to develop additional generalizations. Most, if not all, of the general areas of curriculum engineering that serve as a basic structure to this kind of classification have been indicated in Figure 11 under the content and processes for system maintenance. Briefly the issues are found in: (1) the arena, or arenas in which the various processes of curriculum engineering are to take place, (2) the involvement of people in the curriculum processes, (3) tasks and procedures for curriculum planning, (4) the tasks and procedures for curriculum implementation, and (5) tasks and procedures for curriculum evaluation.

THE ARENA FOR CURRICULUM ENGINEERING

The first decision that has to be reached in establishing a system for curriculum engineering is the arena, or arenas, in which the various curriculum activities are to take place and to be directed. Most subsequent choices are to some degree dependent upon the choice of arena; therefore, it is not a choice to be taken lightly.

Moving from smaller to larger, the most obvious arena choices are the individual school, the school district, the state, and the nation. In the United States, education legally has been a function of the several states. In turn, most state governments have delegated operational control to the various school districts. It has been this act that has resulted in so much autonomy being vested in the hands of local school district officials, including the development of curriculums for the schools. There are, of course, some cases in which state legislatures have passed laws insisting that certain culture content be taught in schools of the state such as teaching about the state constitution, instruction about drug abuse, or a given number of minutes per week to be devoted to physical education. In some states, state departments of education have created suggestive curriculum guides, and they have initiated accountability schemes. But in the main, curriculum decisions have been left to authorities of local school districts. This phenomenon probably accounts for the fact that the most commonly used arena for curriculum planning in the United States is the school district. Occasionally, the authorities of a school district assign curriculum decision making to individual schools. However, the quest for similarity, or uniformity, encourages district authorities to retain responsibility for, and control over, the functions. Until recent years writers and planners have given little thought to the nation as an arena for curriculum decision making, but perhaps the situation is in the act of reversing itself today. As the federal government has invested more heavily in schooling and has expanded its services, individuals have proposed the nation as an arena.

It should be kept in mind that the choice of arena for curriculum engineering encompasses planning, implementation, and evaluation. Depending upon organizational and legal circumstances, it may be necessary to have more than one arena for the three fundamental curriculum engineering processes. For example, a problem of implementation ultimately must be solved at the level of the individual school where the actual persons are present who must develop teaching strategies in response to the curriculum regardless of where the curriculum is planned. In France, for example, the curriculum is planned at the national level under the direction of the Minister of Education, but the curriculum is implemented in the individual schools. In this case, the arena for curriculum planning is the nation; whereas, the arena for implementation is the individual school. On the other hand, if a curriculum is planned in an individual school and implemented in that school, the arena for planning and implementation are the same. It is important to note that the arena decision is very much a prerequisite to other decisions in curriculum engineering. The involvement of people in various types of curriculum decision making and the organization of those people for their various tasks are dependent upon the previous identification of arena.

PERSONNEL INVOLVEMENT

A second group of theoretical issues lies in the selection and involvement of people in the various functions of curriculum engineering, namely, planning, implementation, and evaluation.

Levels of Involvement

Historically at least, four different kinds of persons have been involved in curriculum decision making but mostly in curriculum planning. They are: (1) specialized personnel, (2) representative groups composed of specialized personnel and some classroom teachers, (3) all professional personnel, and (4) all professional personnel plus representative lay citizens. In recent years, a fifth group has been added, namely, the students.

Specialized personnel, in the meaning of the term as used here, refers to at least two groups of people. One consists of persons employed by school districts, or other agencies, specifically to do curriculum work, with the work, in most cases, involving curriculum planning exclusively. These individuals customarily come from the ranks of teachers and supervisors, and they customarily are subject specialists, generalists, or trained curriculum specialists. What makes them specialized personnel is their involvement in curriculum decision-making activities. Schools and school districts have made use of such specialized personnel for many years. The second category, of more recent vintage, consists of persons who are specialized in a discipline and/or who have dominant interest in research in curriculum organization. These people have as their home bases universities or research centers. They rarely work on the total curriculum; instead they concentrate upon the development of a single discipline which may become part of a total curriculum. From time to time, school districts employ them as consultants to help with curriculum development, but they are not in-service curriculum workers in schools. Involvement of specialized personnel in curriculum work was illustrated in the National Curriculum Projects such as the Biological Sciences Curriculum Study, the School Mathematics Study Group, and Project Social Studies. Projects of this type were conducted through the involvement of scholars from the disciplines normally affiliated with universities assisted by selected teachers from elementary and secondary schools.

The involvement of specialized personnel and representative classroom teachers constitutes an extension of the use of specialized personnel. Such involvement assumes that the combination of specialized personnel and representative teacher groups will improve the effectiveness of curriculum decision making. Presumably, it will be improved because of the recency of experience of the teachers in classrooms and because teachers will be able to exert leadership in implementation when the planning is completed. This level of involvement has been used most extensively in large city school systems; Chicago and Los Angeles are two examples. Such selective involvement capitalizes upon the expertise of specialized personnel; it takes advantage of the classroom teacher's point of view, and it is economically efficient in that only a small amount of released time is demanded.

The total involvement of professional personnel as a choice in curriculum engineering is more complicated than the first two. Total involvement means all classroom teachers, supervisors, special teachers, and administrators in a school or a school district. Advocates of this choice of involvement believe that the persons who make curriculum engineering decisions, who develop and execute instructional strategies, and who appraise the various school operations should participate in all three functions. In other words, if teachers and administrators are to participate in the systems of schooling that in this publication have been called the instructional system and the appraisal system, they should also participate in the curriculum system. In reality the only person who actually can participate in all three systems is the teacher; administrators participate by exerting leadership to maintain and improve the systems. The theorist or practitioner who debates and decides on this involvement should know beforehand the teacher-load problems that it carries in its wake. The conventional impression of the job of the teacher is that his sole responsibility is to develop instructional strategies and carry them out with his class or classes. One realizes how strong this impression must be when one observes that teachers in elementary and secondary schools spend almost the entire day in a classroom with pupils trying to carry out predetermined instructional strategies. The development of the strategies must occur outside of the ordinary school day. To think of involving teachers additionally in anything as complicated as a curriculum system as it has been described in the preceding pages appears to be impossible. It is impossible unless ways and means for teachers to participate are found, and the principal ingredient in the ways and means is time unencumbered by teaching responsibility for work on curriculum tasks. Consequently, the two big questions about this choice of involvement are whether one believes that classroom teachers should be involved in curriculum engineering and whether one is willing to develop the ways and means for doing so, assuming the answer to the first question is in the affirmative.

Cooperative lay-professional involvement is an extension of the involvement of all professional personnel inasmuch as the latter are included along with representative lay citizens who have concern about the schools. There is much controversy over the inclusion of lay citizens in curriculum engineering, and many diverse interpretations about the proper role of citizens who are. Those opposed to the involvement claim that because curriculum engineering processes are technical, they should be the sole prerogative of professional groups. Advocates of this position, in contrast, make much of the fundamental authority and responsibility of school patron groups, the extension of the partnership concept in public education, and the improved opportunities that it affords to educate more people in educational concerns. Most of the argument is at the level of value judgment for there is little research on the subject, certainly no comparative research.

Much has been said about the involvement of students in curriculum decisions. The argument is based upon the assertion that if the students are to be affected by the curriculum, they have the right to be involved in deciding what that curriculum should be. Few raise the question of the qualifications of students to make curriculum decisions. For example, is a first-grade pupil equipped to make curriculum decisions for an elementary school? Is a tenth-grade student equipped to make curriculum decisions for a secondary school? It is doubtful in both cases. Yet, one must have great sympathy for the notion that students have had too little involvement in decisions about what they do in schools. I think a distinction needs to be made here between the involvement of students in curriculum planning and the involvement of them in decisions at the level of instruction. Teacher-pupil planning at the level of classroom interaction and decision making has long been advocated. Unfortunately, too little of it has been done. As one result, students can claim that they have been deprived of any real voice in their exposure to schooling. Any posture a curriculum theorist might take on this issue probably depends upon his perception of the scope of curriculum. If he is inclined to think of curriculum strategies and instructional strategies as two related but yet different domains, he will tend to reject the notion of student involvement in curriculum planning. On the other hand, if the theorist is inclined to think of curriculum and instruction as one strategy, he will tend to insist upon student involvement.

Arena and Involvement

It is impossible for anyone to think about the involvement of people in curriculum planning without relating it to the choice, or choices made, or needed to be made, in the arena for curriculum engineering. Any choice of people impinges on the curriculum-engineering arena, and vice versa. Let us take each of the possible arenas and examine the consequences for involvement.

In the case of the national arena, the only possible choice in involvement of people in curriculum planning is that of specialized personnel. It would be possible to include representative teachers, but if the country as a whole were to be represented, a very large group would have to be assembled. To think of total involvement of professional personnel would be ridiculous. However, planning is only one aspect of curriculum engineering. At the level of implementation, all classroom teachers employ the curriculum as a point of departure for their teaching. It would take almost monolithic control at the national level to engineer the implementation of a nationally planned curriculum in the national arena. The only reasonable alternative, in the case of those desiring to use the national arena for curriculum planning, is to split the curriculum engineering functions among two or more arenas. For example, it would be possible to use the national arena for curriculum planning and the individual school as the arena for implementation. We have only to look to France or Italy as illustrations of this type of split in curriculum engineering. In both of these countries, the arena for curriculum planning is the nation; curriculum planning is the responsibility of the national ministers of education. The responsibility for implementing the curriculum in both countries rests with the individual school. The link between the two arenas is the inspector who is the representative of the Minister of Education; it is his responsibility to insure that teachers do, in fact, implement the national curriculum.[1]

We have no similar situation in the United States. Yet individuals and groups at the national level and at regional levels do engage in curriculum activities of various kinds. For instance, scholars of national repute develop materials within their own disciplines. Contributors to curriculum outcomes also consist of scholarly groups such as the National Council for the Social Studies, the National Council of Teachers of English, the American Educational Research Association, the Association for Supervision and Curriculum Development, or the American Association for the Advancement of Science. These organizations prepare and publish materials that are curricular in nature, but they do not prepare total curriculums to be used in schools. They are not part of a curriculum engineering system. However, both the organizations and contributors to their publications influence decisions of those formally involved in the functions of a curriculum engineering system. Their work products actually are input data for a curriculum system.

Because of the delegation of powers over education to school districts by the state governments in the United States, the state has not been extensively used as an arena for curriculum engineering. State departments of education frequently publish curriculum

---

[1]For a more complete analysis of this and other references that will be made to curriculum affairs in Europe, see George A. Beauchamp and Kathryn E. Beauchamp, *Comparative Analysis of Curriculum Systems* (2d ed., Wilmette, Ill.: The Kagg Press, 1972).

guides, but these generally are suggestive only rather than mandates for action in local school districts. In recent years, however, efforts have been made to strengthen the role of state departments of education in matters of leadership over affairs of schooling. The best illustration of these efforts is federal aid to education being administered through the state departments of education. It is not possible for anyone to predict at the moment whether the state actually will emerge as a functional arena for curriculum engineering. If it does, the same general pro and con statements applicable to the nation as an arena relatedly apply to the states. And the same problems of arena splitting and selection of personnel to be involved would persist. In a country such as West Germany, where the state plays the major role in curriculum making, the same problems of personnel involvement and arena choice characteristic of national systems are present.[2]

For all practical purposes, the involvement of personnel in large urban school districts poses the same fundamental problems as it does in a state or the national arena. All professional personnel cannot be involved unless very drastic changes are made in present practices. As indicated before, the most frequently used arena for curriculum planning is the school district, and this applies to large urban centers as it does to small school districts. In the smaller school districts, however, it is possible to totally involve the professional personnel in curriculum planning, and it is also possible to additionally use representative lay citizens. Again, theorists and practitioners have the option of splitting the arena for curriculum engineering by assigning curriculum planning functions to the district arena and the implementation functions to the individual school. Whatever the choice of arena, or arenas, the full range of choices for involvement are available for consideration at the school district level.

The interesting thing about the individual school as the arena for curriculum engineering is that it immediately provides an arena in which all of the curriculum engineering functions may be performed readily. This is particularly true since involvement of teachers in curriculum planning may be followed immediately by involving the same persons in the tasks of curriculum

---

[2]*Ibid.*, pp. 107-125.

implementation. The same persons also remain on the scene to participate in appraisal of the curriculum planning and implementation efforts. An attractive feature of the situation is that the individuals who develop the curriculum strategies are the same ones who develop and carry out the instructional strategies.

An almost immediate reaction from people who seek uniformity among curriculum practices in either the district arena or a larger social-geographic arena is that equal opportunity is denied pupils in schools where curriculum efforts are not "as good" as in others. Caswell, a number of years ago, made the following rejoinder to this argument:

> In brief, the "grass-roots" approach which views the individual school as the operational and planning unit does not mean that each school in a system should go its own way without regard for the others. It means, rather, that problems which are dealt with on a system-wide or partial-system basis should arise out of work done by individual school staffs and feed back into use through these staffs. The channel is from the individual school to the system and back to the individual school rather than from the top down, as under the traditional system-wide approach.[3]

Caswell's statement leads us to propose the ensuing principle: No arena should be completely autonomous in making decisions about curriculum affairs. For example, the individual school cannot be considered as having complete autonomy over its various functions; therefore, curriculum decisions made by higher authority for all schools under the jurisdiction of that authority must be accepted by the individual school unit. If a given state wishes to impose curriculum decisions on all schools and school districts within its borders, it may do so, and all are obliged to abide by those decisions. Nevertheless, the arena for incorporating all of these kinds of decisions into the functional curriculums of the schools remains with the individual school. A similar case could be made for the district as the arena choice. Similarly, the work of scholars in the disciplines and organized scholarly groups may be conceived as influences upon the decisions made in any arena, but the decisions are made only in the operational arena itself.

---

[3]Hollis L. Caswell, *et al., Curriculum Inprovement in Public School Systems* (New York: Bureau of Publications, Teachers College, Columbia University, 1950), p. 78.

CURRICULUM PLANNING

The key function of curriculum engineering is planning. Volumes have been written on the subject of curriculum planning primarily from the point of view of practices in school environments. For the most part, they render advice to those who would become involved in the planning processes. On the other hand those who have addressed themselves to the subject of curriculum theory have not addressed themselves to any significant degree to the theoretical options present within the processes of curriculum planning. In this section, I will cite some exemplars of statements that have been made by curriculum theorists that have bearing upon the subject of curriculum planning. Those exemplars will be followed by a discussion of the theoretical arguments germane to curriculum planning.

Exemplar Statements

Probably the most frequently quoted curriculum rationale was that published by Ralph Tyler in 1950. Tyler proposed as his curriculum rationale four basic questions:

1. What educational purposes should the school seek to attain?
2. What educational experiences can be provided that are likely to attain these purposes?
3. How can these educational experiences be effectively organized?
4. How can we determine whether these purposes are being attained?[4]

The Tyler rationale has been criticized by Kliebard.[5] The details of Kliebard's criticism need not be cited here for they should be read in complete form. Two points do need to be mentioned here, however, for they will have bearing on subsequent discussion. One is the use of the word *experiences* in establishing a rationale for curriculum planning or for purposes of describing curriculum content. As was indicated in Chapter 6, only an individual has an experience, and it is almost impossible for teachers or anyone else to select those experiences. The other point is that although the Tyler rationale does indicate some global movements essential to

---

[4]Ralph W. Tyler, *Basic Principles of Curriculum and Instruction* (Chicago: The University of Chicago Press, 1950) pp. 1-2.

[5]Herbert M. Kliebard, "The Tyler Rationale," *The School Review*, 68:259-272, February, 1970.

curriculum planning, the details of the involvement of people, the arena of decision, and the work procedures are not clarified.

In the development of their rationale for curriculum, Goodlad and Richter identified three levels of curriculum decision making: (1) the societal level, (2) the institutional level, and (3) the instructional level.[6] Presumably, dimensions of curriculum planning take place at all three of these levels. From their discussion, it is not completely clear as to what individuals are to participate at all three of these levels. At the societal level, Goodlad and Richter identify what they call man's funded knowledge and man's conventional wisdom as available for selection as potential curriculum content. The total value system of our society would similarly be available. At the institutional level, the authors indicate that the board of education has predominant control over curriculum decisions. Again, it is not made clear as to how the decisions are made by the board of education, or any other group, at the institutional level. Furthermore, they give virtually no discussion about the transfer from the societal level to the institutional level. It is very clear at the instructional level that teachers are involved in the decision making. By inference, teachers in curriculum decision making at the instructional level would take many of their cues from whatever decision making was made at the institutional level. Exactly when a product appears that is to be called a curriculum is not made clear by Goodlad and Richter, but it is clear that the final step is at the instructional level. It is interesting to note here that it is possible that Goodlad and Richter have conceived of groups of individuals involved in curriculum decision making who have no direct contact with one another. It is also clear that instructional planning, in their judgment, is a part of the total curriculum process. The techniques of curriculum planning were omitted. Presumably, they were not considered important for fulfilling the authors' avowed purpose to set forth a curriculum rationale.

Taba recognized and described most of the generally accepted procedures for curriculum development, namely, the process of determining objectives, selecting content expected to facilitate the

---

[6]John I. Goodlad and Maurice N. Richter, Jr., *The Development of a Conceptual System for Dealing with Problems of Curriculum and Instruction* (Los Angeles: Institute for Development of Educational Activities, University of California, 1966).

achievement of goals, and the development of an evaluation procedure. She did, however, reverse the more or less commonly accepted procedure by suggesting that instead of developing a general plan for the school program as an initial step, it would be more profitable to start with the planning of teaching-learning units. In such a scheme, units would provide a basis for the general design.[7] The steps that she proposed for development of a teaching-learning unit were: diagnosing needs, formulating specific objectives, selecting content, organizing content, selecting and organizing learning experiences, evaluating and checking for balance and sequence.[8] The procedures suggested by Taba seems to reverse the order of the two systems of schooling, curriculum and instruction. In other words, the curriculum would emerge from the instructional strategies. In their model of the process of curriculum planning, Saylor and Alexander included curriculum determinants which guide curriculum planners who make curriculum decisions which result in curriculum planning at several levels: the nation, the state, the school system, the school, the teaching group, and the individual teacher.[9] Purportedly, decisions made at each step affect subsequent decisions as the decision-making functions shift from state to individual teacher, with national efforts having influence along the line.

Theoretical Issues

The foregoing examples of statements about curriculum planning and decision making are illustrative of different choices made by their authors with respect to the dimensions of curriculum planning. For example, they illustrate vividly the problems associated with the selection of an arena for curriculum planning and the involvement of people in the planning process. Raising the question about what the arena shall be for curriculum planning specifically points us toward a time from which there must emerge a product to be called a curriculum. The fact that authors indicate that curriculum planning is done at various levels such as the

---

[7]Hilda Taba, *Curriculum Development: Theory and Practice* (New York: Harcourt, Brace and World, Inc., 1962), pp. 441-442.

[8]*Ibid.*, pp. 347-379.

[9]J. Galen Saylor and William M. Alexander, *Planning Curriculum for Schools* (New York: Holt, Rinehart and Winston, Inc., 1974), p. 52.

societal level, the institutional level, the classroom level, the state level, the school level, or the teacher level, to cite examples, indicates that the authors simply do not expect anything resembling a curriculum to emerge from any one of those levels. If we are going to talk about curriculum planning, it would seem reasonable that a primary decision that must be made is the arena level from which it is expected that a curriculum will emerge. The dilemma that is posed by arguments suggesting that curriculum decisions are made at several levels perhaps may be resolved by deciding at which point decisions about what to teach in schools are transmitted to those who must make decisions about how to teach the results of the first decision. In that case, any decisions affecting the curriculum that would appear at a previous or a higher level of decision making would be considered as inputs to the process of curriculum planning. It seems ridiculous to assume that we can have a national curriculum, a state curriculum, a school curriculum, a classroom curriculum, or an individual curriculum, all at the same time. If we had all of these curricula, it would be extremely difficult to differentiate which of them was to be implemented in the classrooms.

Organization of people to carry out curriculum planning procedures is dependent upon both the arena chosen for doing the curriculum planning and the kind and number of people involved in the planning activity. The problems and choices available to the theorist are not extensive when specialists are involved in curriculum planning, because specialists tend to be very few in number. Furthermore, they tend to work as a whole, devising their own unique ways of working together. Organization for curriculum planning becomes critical, however, when large and diversified numbers of people are involved. The complexities thus created constitute the theme of the following paragraphs.

One of the choices in organizing personnel to engage in curriculum planning was associated in the previous discussion with large urban centers or cities. This choice is a central office staff of curriculum specialists who have the principal responsibility for action and leadership in curriculum planning. To this group may be added representatives of the classroom teacher group, administrators, outside consultants, and/or representative lay citizens. The most common practice is for cities or large districts to organize the individuals involved into subject committees to prepare curriculum guides for the assigned subjects. Each committee tends to work independently, with the result that the total curriculum is an accumulation of separate-subject pamphlets. A schedule for revision of the guides is usually established so that they are revised every three, four, or five years. Committees are disbanded when the planning task is completed, and new ones created at the time of the next revision. Havighurst reported on a system of this type for the city of Chicago.[10]

In the small school district or the individual school arena, more possibilities for organizational schemes are apparent. In these arenas, it is feasible for curriculum engineers to involve all professional personnel and selected representative lay citizens if desired. The rule that must apply in this kind of circumstance is to create organization that will serve best the functions that have to be performed. It is common practice for curriculum planning groups to be headed by a curriculum council or a steering committee. Under such an arrangement, the council has the authority to organize groups and to reconstitute them as experience demands change.

Beauchamp reported studies of the effects of curriculum engineering in an elementary school district in Blue Island, Illinois.[11] For curriculum planning purposes, all teachers were organized into vertical and horizontal committees. The vertical committees were composed of teachers representing all grades, and each committee was assigned to a particular school subject. Horizontal committees were grade level committees. Their responsibility was to study the problems of horizontal articulation among subjects. The vertical and horizontal planning committees were headed by a curriculum council. The curriculum council consisted of the chairman of the vertical and horizontal committees. In this system, the curriculum is subject to revision each school year. It is an interesting example of curriculum planning being done on a school district level in a relatively small district.

---

[10]Robert J. Havighurst, *The Public Schools of Chicago* (Chicago: The Board of Education of the City of Chicago, 1964), pp. 98-117.

[11]Mimeographed papers presented at annual meetings of the American Educational Research Association in 1972, 1973, and 1974.

It is extremely difficult to identify the use of the individual school arena as a base for curriculum planning in the United States. This would not be true in England, for example, where virtually all curriculum decisions are made at the individual school level even though other organizations may exist that would have some effect upon the decisions made at the individual school level.

The two major functions served by organization are to insure representation of all essential groups and to facilitate the tasks to be done. When the arena is the school district, all schools and all divisions in those schools may be represented on work committees or groups. Total involvement does not mean that all persons have to be involved in all specific tasks, but the organization must be such that all feel that they have been involved either through their own participation or through the participation of colleagues in whom they have faith to carry their share of the burden. No halo surrounds any particular organizing scheme because in tasks as complicated as those involved in curriculum planning no single scheme is consistently appropriate. Diverse curriculum groups and committees may be formed, including, for instance, study groups, discussion groups, consultant groups, leadership groups, subject committees, departmental committees, grade-level committees, system-wide committees, school committees, special committees, editing committees, coordinating committees, and so forth. Such groups and committees are constituted, disbanded, or reconstituted depending upon need.

From the point of view of theory building with respect to curriculum planning, organization is dependent to a large extent on the arena chosen for conducting the planning and the degree of involvement of people within the arena. Choices among the options must be consistent in order to adequately explain the necessary series of events. For example, to begin with the state as a chosen area for curriculum planning and to opt for total teacher involvement in the planning would be to create a situation in which organization and assignment of tasks would be impossible. On the other hand, to use a small district as the arena and to opt for total teacher involvement in the planning would be to create a situation in which organization and assignment of tasks would be highly feasible.

Procedures or techniques in curriculum planning are specifically related to the tasks involved. Most of the procedures in curriculum planning are relatively simple. They involve such processes as group discussion, study of relevant information, and writing. These procedures will vary somewhat according to the tasks involved. The principal tasks in curriculum planning vary according to whether the planning group is undertaking curriculum planning for the first time or whether the planning process is part of an ongoing curriculum engineering scheme. The basic tasks, however, are: to seek and receive information, to filter and organize the information, to create ideas for curriculum change, to select a curriculum design, to write the curriculum, to check for vertical and horizontal articulation, and to submit the curriculum to the appropriate authority for acceptance and approval. Some discussion of each of these is warranted.

It has often been said that teachers are not qualified or capable of participating in curriculum planning, and in many cases, teachers have expressed a similar feeling of inadequacy. Quips have been made that teacher involvement in curriculum planning is essentially a process of pooling of ignorance. Yet those very same teachers are expected to have the necessary insight to take a curriculum planned by someone else and implement it intelligently in their classrooms. One answer to this dilemma is to treat curriculum planning within a school district as a regular part of the in-service education of teachers by involving them in receiving and seeking out information so they can do a better job of the curriculum planning. In Figure 11, there were listed examples of input data for the curriculum system in a school. It is exactly this input information that curriculum planning groups need to receive as background data for making curriculum decisions.

An important subsequent task is to filter and organize the input information in such a way that it becomes useful to the planners. This is not a trite step and it is one that is frequently overlooked. For example, a consultant may be used for such purposes as suggesting new social studies content for the curriculum. If the receiving, or planning, group does nothing other than listen to those ideas as presented by a consultant, the planning group probably will not be greatly affected by the use of the consultant. If the members of a planning group receive information by listening to a consultant, by reading, or by input from one another, they then should have the opportunity to discuss the character of the input information and to weigh the consequences of preferred suggestions for them. This is a task that should not be short circuited in terms of the amount of time spent on it. The combination of the receipt of information and the organization of that information for use is probably one of the most important steps of curriculum planning. One may think of the tasks of seeking and receiving information and the filtering and organizing of the information as composing the study phase of curriculum planning. Logically, the next task in curriculum planning would be to select a curriculum design. If a curriculum is already in existence, the planning group may be prone to maintain the same design. On the other hand, the ideas that had been created for inclusion as a result of the study phase may indicate a needed change in the existing design. The options with respect to curriculum design are relatively few. Most of them were described in the previous chapter focused upon the subject of curriculum design. We still find that the subject-centered organization of culture content in curriculums predominates. There are attempts at more integrated organization. Occasionally, a combination of those two may be indicated. Planners should keep in mind that one purpose of curriculum planning is to render advice to teachers as they proceed in the development of instructional strategies. If the curriculum cannot be used for this purpose, we should raise grave doubts about the need for creating one in the first place. The model of the processes of curriculum planning, followed by the processes of instructional planning, followed by the processes of teaching and learning, followed by evaluation in order to acquire information about how to improve various elements of that cycle the next time around are very important.

When the design has been selected, the planning group or groups may then proceed to write the curriculum. The procedures for doing so may depend greatly upon the organization. Where committees have been used for purposes of receiving and analyzing information and for creating new ideas for curriculum change, those same committees may be used as writing groups at this step. On the other hand, special writing committees may have to be created because of the complexity of committee organization.

In any case, whatever is written needs to be approved by all participants in the planning process. The processes of creating ideas for curriculum change, selecting a curriculum design, and writing the curriculum may be spoken of as the creating phase of curriculum planning.

Once the curriculum has been written it needs to be very carefully checked for vertical and horizontal articulation of goals and culture content. It would include articulation between subjects if the culture content is so organized. It would include a search for opportunities to integrate various components of culture content for purposes of efficiency and learning on the part of the students. And it would involve any reworking or rewriting of the curriculum based upon the checking procedure. It should be kept in mind that change in curriculum may be instituted at any level or in any program within the curriculum so long as the planners recognize that a change in one place may have an effect on other places in the curriculum. This is the real reason for including an opportunity for checking for vertical and horizontal articulation within the total curriculum planning process.

Once the curriculum has been written and properly checked, it then needs to be submitted for approval and acceptance to whatever authority constituted the planning groups in the first place. Where special project groups may have been involved in curriculum planning, they are normally allowed the privilege of acceptance and approval by themselves, with the possible exception of the approval of some sponsoring group such as a supporting foundation. In the vast majority of cases in public schools, the curriculum is essential policy of the board of education. Hence, the board of education becomes the agency to approve and accept as their policy a new curriculum or any curriculum previously approved that has been modified. The acts of checking for vertical and horizontal articulation and for acceptance and approval may be spoken of as the checking phase of curriculum planning.

The foregoing tasks and procedures incorporate most of the tasks and functions proposed by curriculum authorities as well as those that have been used in projects reported by school systems. Variations will reflect unique ways of working within whatever frameworks groups have discovered to be effective for them. Most groups who undertake a curriculum planning project need to search for and to develop their own unique ways of working together to achieve their mutually accepted goals. Unquestionably, it is difficult for anyone to transplant specific procedures from persons and curriculum situations detached in time and place. Yet the basic tasks remain the same.

Other than involvement of people, there are no great theoretical issues regarding curriculum planning. In other words, who shall do curriculum planning is more controversial than how they shall do it. What is needed is empirical research on task and method variables in curriculum planning to set the stage for concrete theoretical issues to be created.

CURRICULUM IMPLEMENTATION

Curriculum implementation means putting the curriculum to work. The two most justifiable reasons for a curriculum are as a point of departure for teaching and as an initial system for predicting outcomes. Curriculum implementation, in effect, consists of the processes necessary .to accomplish these two purposes.

The first task in curriculum implementation is to arrange the school environment in such a way that the curriculum is used by teachers as a point of departure for their teaching. As indicated in Figure 10 at the beginning of this chapter, implementation takes place during the spacetime representing the merger of the curriculum system with the instructional system. At this point, the curriculum becomes a working tool for teachers as they develop their instructional strategies. This is the point where the message of the curriculum planner is communicated to and interpreted by the teacher for a specific group, or for groups, of pupils. For a school to accomplish these ends, an agreed upon course of action needs to be determined and accepted by those who are to implement the curriculum. Assessment of changes in pupil behavior cannot be made until instruction takes place, but the planning of instructional strategy is an extension of the planned curriculum strategy. Both strategies seek outcomes which can only be brought to light subsequent to the teaching-learning activities.

Our history of curriculum implementation is weak. Many curriculums have been planned, but few have been systematically implemented. We are all familiar with the circumstances in which the curriculum, once it is produced, collects dust on a shelf or is filed in the bottom right-hand drawer of the teacher's desk. In the meantime, the teacher reverts to the same pattern of teaching that he used prior to the planning of the curriculum. Curriculum planning under these circumstances is a tremendous waste of human effort except for the concomitant educational gains for the planners.

A necessary prerequisite for curriculum implementation is the commitment by teachers to use the curriculum as a point of departure for development of instructional strategies. The strength of the commitment may be enhanced by an implementation directive being part of the curriculum, teacher participation in the curriculum planning, and administrative leadership. This is why the proposal was made in Chapter 6 that one section of a curriculum should be a clear statement of the use to be made of it. The statement may register the commitment and provide suggested procedures for implementation. We have had little experience with similar modes of recording in the United States, so specific illustrations are difficult to find. The schools of Italy, however, offer a very concrete illustration. In the new Italian middle school, a very systematic procedure is used. The curriculum for the middle school is established by Parliament and the Minister of Public Instruction; all middle schools have the same curriculum. The curriculum is not an elaborate document, but it is clear as to what subjects are to be taught, the general range of each subject for each class, and the amount of time per week to be devoted to each subject. But along with the curriculum are instructions for implementation and adaptation. Each teacher is required to adapt the curriculum to his particular group of pupils, and furthermore, is required to demonstrate that he has done so. An elaborate system of forms and registers is provided for these purposes, and inspectors review these documents to determine if the curriculum has been followed and if the implementation procedures have been executed.[12] The implementation

---

[12]See Beauchamp and Beauchamp, *op. cit.*, Chapter IV.

procedures used in Italy would not mesh well with most practices in the United States, but they do illustrate how a planned curriculum may include provisions for implementation.

Curriculum implementation is facilitated if teachers who are to use the curriculum participate in its planning. Involvement, in effect, leads to follow through. This outcome was attested to by Johansen when he concluded that both individual teacher participation in curriculum planning activities and perception by teachers that they were influential in curriculum decision making increased the likelihood of curriculum implementation.[13] Duet used the same inventories that Johansen used and came to similar conclusions.[14] His results showed a significant relationship between teacher participation on curriculum committees and their implementation practices. In a study of teacher attitudes, Langenbach found a significant difference in attitude of teachers toward curriculum use and planning between those who had participated in curriculum planning and those who had not.[15] Somewhat similar conclusions were reached by Heusner[16] and Nault,[17] but they cautioned against assuming that participation in curriculum planning alone would insure implementation. Other conditions are needed to support implementation efforts. For example, Poll noted a significant relationship between teacher use of curriculums and the help they received in that use.[18] Like Johansen, Kardas found a significant relationship between implementation practices of teachers and their satisfaction with teaching as a profession.[19]

[13]Johansen, John H., "An Investigation of the Relationships between Teachers' Perceptions of Authoritative Influences in Local Curriculum Decision-Making and Curriculum Implementation" (Doctoral dissertation, Northwestern University, Evanston, Illinois, 1965).

[14]Claude Paul Duet, Jr., "The Relationship of Teacher Participation on Curriculum Committees to Implementation of Curriculum Guides and Materials" (Doctoral dissertation, University of Georgia, 1972).

[15]Michael Langenbach, "The Development of an Instrument to Measure Teachers' Attitudes toward Curriculum Use and Planning" (Doctoral dissertation, Northwestern University, Evanston, Illinois, 1969).

[16]Henry C. Heusner, "A Study of the Utilization of Curriculum Guides as Related to Selection Factors in their Planning and Construction" (Doctoral dissertation, Wayne State University, Detroit, Michigan, 1963).

[17]William H. Nault, "Can Curriculum Guides be Effective?" *Educational Leadership*, 12:410-424, April, 1965.

[18]Diana Poll, "A Study of Selected Factors Related to the Implementation of Centrally Prepared Curriculum Guides" (Doctoral dissertation, Northwestern University, Evanston, Illinois, 1970).

[19]Barbara J. Kardas, "Characteristics of Teacher Participation in Curriculum Planning Activities and Reported Acts of Curriculum Implementation" (Doctoral dissertation, Northwestern University, Evanston, Illinois, 1969).

Since the principle of teacher involvement seems so self-evident, the question arises as to why teachers are not routinely required to participate in curriculum planning in most schools. The reasons offered by opponents of the principle generally carry considerable weight. One is that most teachers are not qualified to make curriculum decisions; that high caliber specialists in the various disciplines alone can do the job properly. Another is that teachers do not have time to devote to the time-consuming tasks of curriculum planning and development because their full work days are consumed with the execution of instructional strategies, and they should not be concerned with planning the curriculum. What is needed is more carefully designed research to provide valid and reliable data, such as that cited previously by Johansen and others, leading to generalizations that will permit choices about involvement as it affects both the outcomes of planning and the processes of implementation.

The degree to which teachers lack commitment to the curriculum that has been planned constitutes a potential barrier to curriculum implementation. Teachers may feel that the curriculum is inappropriate for their students, or they may claim that the curriculum is too rigid, or they may claim that materials of instruction, including textbooks, are not available to implement the curriculum properly. For such reasons, teachers are prone to fear the imposition of a curriculum as a point of departure for developing their teaching strategies. Peculiarly enough, the same fear has not been associated with the adopted textbooks even though they may be just as restrictive as any planned curriculum. The challenge here is for curriculum planners to create designs that are not rigid and to institute realistic implementation procedures.

Ability grouping practices in schools point to the question of need for separate curriculums for groups which differ on one or many dimensions. It was reported in the Havighurst survey of the Chicago public schools that many teachers claimed that the planned curriculum was not appropriate for pupils in their classes and schools.[20] In this connection, Larson did a carefully controlled study of acts of implementation by both inner-city and outer-city

---

[20]*Op. cit.*

primary teachers in an urban school district wherein a commonly prescribed curriculum was used. Among the factors observed were the number of omissions and the number of additions made to the prescribed curriculum by teachers in both types of schools. Larson concluded that inner-city teachers tend to make more omissions than outer-city teachers, that outer-city teachers tend to make more additions than inner-city teachers, and that inner-city teachers tend to give less overall coverage to the curriculum than do outer-city teachers.[21] In attempts to solve this problem of pupil differences, a number of school systems are planning curriculums for two or three pupil groups, such as a normal group, an upper ability group, and a low ability disadvantaged group. Is the need for multiple curriculums lessened if the curriculum planning arena is the individual school? Is the need increased if a larger arena than the individual school is used for curriculum planning? What effect does involvement of teachers in curriculum planning have upon the problem? Little hard-nosed research is available to provide answers to the above questions. At present they are being answered subjectively by those responsible for making curriculum decisions, and we cannot fault this practice in most situations. A well-organized system for curriculum engineering, however, would make the answers more valid.

A consideration that is omitted too frequently from a discussion of the problems of curriculum implementation is the role of administrative personnel. The prognosis for successful implementation of a curriculum is weak when administrators are indifferent to its importance. Conversely, the prognosis is strong when administrators share with teachers the importance of the curriculum being implemented systematically. Implementation is facilitated when administrative personnel accept the roles of chief engineers of the system and act accordingly.

Ultimately, the teacher is the person who must implement a curriculum, but collectively teachers will not implement the curriculum solely on their own initiative. The exercise of leadership is critical for a systematic implementation of any curriculum. In the United States the school principal is the most

---

[21]Richard G. Larson, "The Implementation of an Urban School Curriculum by Inner-city and Outer-city Primary Teachers: A Comparative Study of Deviations from Prescribed Curricula" (Doctoral dissertation, Northwestern University, Evanston, Illinois, 1968).

likely person to be charged with the leadership responsibility. In her previously cited study, Conran observed a strong relationship between a principal's leadership effectiveness and the perceptions of his teachers of their performance in a curriculum system. Similarly, a strong relationship was noted between a principal's leadership and his students' achievement in the various subject areas.

The principal, or anyone else charged with the leadership, is greatly assisted if there is provision in the curriculum itself for the curriculum implementation process. This need not be lengthy, but it should contain the generally accepted directions people are to follow with respect to implementation. Functionally, the processes of implementation set the stage for any subsequent efforts to improve instruction. Basically the implementation process is one of making a transition between the curriculum plan and the teaching plan.

There are few, if any, theoretical issues with regard to curriculum implementation. The processes of curriculum implementation are not materially affected by curriculum design. That is, it makes little difference whether a curriculum contains simply statements of goals and culture content selected to achieve those goals or whether those are also accompanied with entries having to do with instructional matters. In either case, the curriculum must be implemented. Any curriculum must be implemented, else we have justification for raising questions as to why it should have been planned in the first place. One might argue about the leadership responsibility because that may vary from system to system. In national systems such as France and Italy, for instance, the Minister of Education's inspectors are responsible for the implementation effort. For the most part in the United States, school principals are responsible. There also may be the special case of specially appointed supervisory personnel being delegated that responsibility.

CURRICULUM EVALUATION

Although curriculum evaluation is rightfully a part of the total appraisal system of schooling, the execution of the evaluative aspects of curriculum functionally must be part of the curriculum system and therefore subject to curriculum engineering. There are at least four dimensions of curriculum evaluation: (1) evaluation of teacher use of curriculum, (2) evaluation of the design, (3) evaluation of pupil outcomes, and (4) evaluation of the curriculum system. Experience with these four dimensions is very limited; therefore, most of what can be said about them has to be logically inferred.

Evaluation of teacher use is logically a first step in curriculum evaluation, and it is a step that is almost universally overlooked in curriculum evaluation. The most simple data on teacher use are observations of the number of teachers who actually use the curriculum as a point of departure for developing their teaching strategies. When teachers do not use the curriculum from which to develop their teaching strategies, curriculum evaluation stops at that point. Any evaluation done under these circumstances cannot be termed curriculum evaluation. Among the more plausible reasons for non-use are that teachers are unable or unwilling to develop supporting teaching strategies; teachers do not feel that they can or should depart from an adopted textbook; or they feel that the curriculum is not an adequate one. Conversely, evidence showing use of the curriculum as a point of departure by all teachers for developing teaching strategies constitutes convincing evidence about the dynamic quality of the curriculum. Quality of the use made is another matter. Possible indications of this are the additions, omissions, and adaptations effected to meet the differing needs of learners. Another consists of the kind of feedback for replanning groups furnished by teachers because of their experiences with the curriculum. Another, but a very difficult one to measure in any sense, is the enthusiasm of teachers for participating in the curriculum system to the extent of making systematic use of the curriculum for developing instructional plans.

Evaluation of curriculum design is very difficult because of absence of criteria for doing so. Different designs are not available to be compared and matched against common criteria. To be sure, the success of teachers in the use of a curriculum, as described in the previous paragraph, would have evaluative implications for the adequacy of the design. So would the success of the predictions inherent in the curriculum for pupil learning outcomes. Other criteria specifically related to design questions should direct the major aspects of the evaluation of curriculum design, but those criteria have yet to be formulated.

Although we have not learned much about how to compare curriculum design A with curriculum design B with adequate research controls, we can evaluate individual parts of a design. Goals and/or objectives are an example. When more general goals are stated in a curriculum, Grotelueschen and Gooler would argue for the establishment of priorities for goals as part of the curriculum evaluation.[22] Certainly the Delphi Technique, or some modification of it, should be helpful in this task. If a curriculum contains specific behavioral objectives, their clarity is an important criterion for evaluation, but the real test of behavioral objectives is as predictors of student learning. In fact, the greatest justification for specific behavioral objectives in preference for the more general goals statements may be that the predictive leap to measurement of learnings is easier to make. Another evaluation focus point is the relationship between goals and the culture content selected as means for achieving those goals. Curriculum students repeatedly report lack of clear relationships between goals and culture content in curriculum materials they have reviewed. If such observations are at all accurate, more careful evaluation of the relationship is needed during the curriculum planning process. Similarly, logical criteria may be used to make judgments about the culture content. Relevance is one. Psychological fit to the learners is another. Balance between substantive and syntactical content is a third. Many more could be added to these; thus, even though we have had little or no experience in evaluating curriculum design, we can begin with parts and work toward the whole.

Of the four approaches to curriculum evaluation, assessment of the curriculum as an instrument to predict pupil outcomes is the most difficult to attain. The reason is that the many variables of the entire instructional system of schooling intervene (necessarily so, of course) between the time of curriculum planning and the observance of pupil learnings. At the level of appraising student learnings, we should discriminate between intended learnings and learnings acquired outside the realms of curriculum and

---

[22]Arden D. Grotelueschen and Dennis D. Gooler, "Evaluation in Curriculum Development" *Curriculum Theory Network*, 8/9:7-21, 1971/72.

instruction. If the curriculum is a basic plan with intended goals and culture content selected that is expected to produce those goals, and if instructional planning has expanded them into specific objectives, those goals should be the bases for appraisal of the deliberate efforts of the school. The school may take credit for such learnings. On the other hand, school pupils have many learning opportunities both in and out of school that contribute to their total learning growth, but those learnings are not the product of deliberate thinking by curriculum planners and instructional strategists. This distinction is not to denigrate those learnings acquired outside the deliberate framework. They may be as worthwhile as the learnings deliberately fostered, and they may considerably affect the learnings fostered through instruction. Certainly, all learnings contribute to the total behavior of the individual, and the school should be as aware of the total mass as appraisal techniques will permit. Unless both categories are taken into account, the school has little basis for being credited with the production of pupil learning. This also helps to make the idea of measures of achievement as a sole criterion for judging the effectiveness of schools, or a curriculum, very faulty.

Every aspect of the curriculum system must be brought under the microscope of evaluation, or the system deteriorates from lack of vitality. Feedback from the evaluation of the system must be available to rejuvenate the system's parts. The choice of arena, the choices made for involvement, organization of people for work, work procedures, and roles played by leadership personnel are all subjects to be appraised for strengths and weaknesses. These are the functions that make a curriculum system work. The feedback from evaluation of them helps to improve the system and to provide for continuity and growth from year to year.

A full range of techniques of measurement and appraisal is called for in curriculum evaluation. However, not all evidence produced by curriculum evaluation will be in quantitative form. Substantial evidence will be the subjective opinions of teachers which are rival in any scheme of curriculum evaluation. The number and kind of recommendations for change is useful information for making judgments about the system. Our experience with curriculum evaluation is meager, and there is great need for curriculum workers to begin collecting all kinds of evidence to judge the worth of planned curriculums and curriculum systems.

SUMMARY AND A POINT OF VIEW

Summary

A curriculum system is a system for decision making and action with respect to curriculum functions. A curriculum system has three primary functions: (1) to produce a curriculum, (2) to implement a curriculum, and (3) to appraise the effectiveness of a curriculum and a curriculum system. Curriculum engineering consists of all the processes and activities necessary to maintain and improve a curriculum system including leadership by such chief engineers as the superintendent, the principal, and the curriculum director.

In this chapter, the term schooling has been employed to cover those activities essential in the purposeful maintenance and operation of schools. Three of the more important systems of schooling were identified as the curriculum, the instructional, and the evaluation systems. Our major concern is with the curriculum system. However, the interrelationships among the various systems serve to explain curriculum theory.

The language of systems analysis is applicable for describing a curriculum system. Input data for a curriculum system are derived primarily from educational foundations and past experience in curriculum affairs. The primary functions to be served by the content and processes of the system are to get a curriculum planned, to get it implemented through an instructional system, and to get it modified as a result of evaluative feedback. The most tangible and the most important output of a curriculum system is a curriculum.

It is in the engineering of the various activities of the curriculum system that the most apparent theoretical issues emerge. The choice of arena for curriculum engineering from the nation, the state, the district, or the school is fundamental. Curriculum engineering can function in any one or in any combination of these arenas. It is possible to divide the total arena for curriculum engineering into two parts depending upon function. For example, one arena may be used for curriculum planning, and another may be used for curriculum implementation. When the arena is thus split, curriculum evaluation may take place in either of the arenas or in both.

Exactly who is to be involved in curriculum decision making constitutes an important consideration of curriculum engineering. The most obvious choices are specialized personnel, representative specialists and teachers, all professional personnel, and all professional personnel plus representative lay citizens. There is very close relationship between choice of arena and choice of people to be involved.

Two basic considerations dictate organization and procedures for curriculum planning. One is the size of the group to be involved in the planning, and the other is the number of tasks or steps that are to be undertaken. The complexity of organization increases as groups become larger. Curriculum planning by large groups is too complex for there to be permanent task groups, with the possible exception of the curriculum council or the steering committee. Procedures tend to dictate organization, and, in turn, tasks tend to dictate many procedures.

Curriculum implementation consists of the processes necessary to get the curriculum used as a point of departure for developing teaching strategies. Regardless of choices made concerning arena or involvement for planning, the classroom teacher is the only person who can do the implementing. Consequently, teacher commitment to do so is fundamental to success in implementation. In this connection, teacher participation in curriculum planning is one of the most successful devices for eliciting the commitment. Barriers to implementation include lack of commitment, feelings by teachers that a curriculum is inappropriate for pupils, and lack of leadership by administrative personnel.

Curriculum evaluation involves evaluating teacher use of the curriculum, the design, pupil outcome predictions, and the curriculum system. Limited experience in this area points up the drastic need for case studies and research that will lead to suggested procedures and theoretical generalizations.

A Point of View

Again, I shall use my own position to illustrate how a theorist might select from the issues that have been summarized above so as to establish a consistent position with respect to curriculum engineering. As background for this position on curriculum engineering, several things need to be kept in mind. In the first place, I choose to use the word curriculum only in three ways: (1) to refer to a curriculum, (2) to refer to a curriculum system, or (3) to refer to curriculum as a field of study. Curriculum engineering is product-oriented in that the principal concern in curriculum engineering is the planning of the curriculum, its implementation, and its evaluation. I consider a curriculum as a plan for a school or a class of school such as an elementary school, a junior high school, or a senior high school. Optimally, a curriculum will contain at least four parts: (1) a statement describing how the curriculum is intended to be used, (2) a set of goal statements, (3) a body of culture content selected as means for achieving the previously stated goals, and (4) an evaluation scheme that sets the stage for continuous curriculum revision. With this background we can discuss my position with respect to the dimensions of curriculum engineering.

The first dimension is that of the arena within which curriculum functions are to take place. Among the choices available, I would select the individual school as the most desirable arena for both curriculum planning and implementation. The individual school is a group of professionals under the leadership of a prinicpal. These people are in a face-to-face relationship each day. This set of circumstances provides optimal conditions for developing consistent points of view for such functions as curriculum planning and implementation. The individual school is the place where curriculum implementation must ultimately take place regardless of where it is planned. There currently is sufficient research evidence to lead us to the generalization that for maximum curriculum implementation the curriculum should be planned by those who are to implement it. The choice of the individual school as an arena does not eliminate from consideration or influence any of the other arenas. The district or the state may lay down controls or minimum standards for what

I have three concerns with respect to curriculum evaluation. The first concern has to do with whether teachers actually do use the curriculum as a guide for instructional planning. The second has to do with the predictive effect of the curriculum upon the achievement of students in accordance with stated aims or purposes, and the third has to do with the results of the evaluation upon the planning function. These concerns are unique to the persons and the situation of individual schools; consequently, every school will have to devise its own means for dealing with these important matters. There are no established procedures.

SUGGESTED READINGS

American Educational Research Association. "Curriculum Planning and Development," *Review of Educational Research*, 27:237-304, June, 1957.

American Educational Research Association. "Curriculum Planning and Development," *Review of Educational Research*, 30:181-279, June, 1960.

American Educational Research Association. "Curriculum Planning and Development," *Review of Educational Research*, 33:227-337, June, 1963.

American Educational Research Association. "Curriculum Planning and Development," *Review of Educational Research*, 36:339-389, June, 1966.

American Educational Research Association. "Curriculum," *Review of Educational Research*, 39:283-375, June, 1969.

Ammons, Margaret and Robert S. Gilchrist. *Assessing and Using Curriculum Content* Washington, D. C.: the Association for Supervision and Curriculum Development, NEA, 1965.

Anderson, Dan W., James B. Macdonald, and Frank B. May (eds.). *Strategies of Curriculum Development*. Columbus: Charles E. Merrill Books, Inc., 1965.

Anderson, Vernon, E. *Principles and Procedures of Curriculum Development*. 2d ed. New York: The Ronald Press Company, 1965.

Association for Supervision and Curriculum Development, NEA. *Curriculum Change: Direction and Process*. Washington, D.C.: the Association, 1966.

Association for Supervision and Curriculum Development, NEA. *What are the Sources of the Curriculum? A Symposium*. Washington, D.C.: the Association, 1962.

Beauchamp, George A. "Basic Components of a Curriculum Theory," *Curriculum Theory Network*, Toronto, Ontario: The Ontario Institute for Studies in Education, Fall, 1972, pp. 16-22.

Beauchamp, George A. *The Curriculum of the Elementary School*. Boston: Allyn and Bacon, Inc., 1964.

Beauchamp, George A. *Curriculum Theory*. 2d ed. Wilmette, Illinois: The Kagg Press, 1968.

Beauchamp, George A. and Kathryn E. Beauchamp. *Comparative Analysis of Curriculum Systems*. 2d ed. Wilmette, Ill.: The Kagg Press, 1972.

Clark, Leonard H., Raymond L. Klein, and John B. Burks. *The American Secondary School Curriculum*. 2d ed. New York: The Macmillan Company, 1972.

Conner, Forrest E. and William J. Ellena (eds.). *Curriculum Handbook for School Administrators*. Washington, D.C.: American Association of School Administrators, NEA, 1967.

Conran, Patricia C. "A Study of Causal and Other Relationships among Leadership, Teacher, and Student Variables in Curriculum Engineering." Doctoral dissertation, Northwestern University, Evanston, Illinois, 1974.

Dahllöf, Urban S. *Ability Grouping, Content Validity, and Curriculum Process Analysis*. New York: Teachers College Press, Teachers College, Columbia University, 1971.

Doll, Ronald C. *Curriculum Improvement: Decision-Making and Process*. 2d ed. Boston: Allyn and Bacon, Inc., 1970.

Faunce, Roland C. and Nelson L. Bossing. *Developing the Core Curriculum*. 2d ed. Englewood Cliffs, N.J.: Prentice-Hall, Inc., 1958.

Firth, Gerald R. and Richard D. Kimpston. *The Curricular Continuum in Perspective*. Itasca, Ill.: F.E. Peacock Publishers, Inc., 1973.

Goodkind, Thomas Barrett. "A Study of the Impact of the Illinois Curriculum Program Upon Local School District Curriculum Operations." Doctoral dissertation, Northwestern University, Evanston, Illinois, 1965.

Gwynn, J. Minor and John Chase. *Curriculum Principles and Social Trends*. 4th ed. New York: The Macmillan Company, 1969.

Hass, Glenn, Joseph Bondi and Jon Wiles. *Curriculum Planning: A new Approach*. Rockleigh, New Jersey: College Division, Allyn and Bacon, Inc., 1974.

Inlow, Gail M. *The Emergent in Curriculum*. 2d ed. New York: John Wiley and Sons, Inc., 1973.

Johansen, John H. "The Relationships between Teachers' Perceptions of Influence in Local Curriculum Decision-Making and Curriculum Implementation," *The Journal of Educational Research*, 61:81-83, October, 1967.

Kardas, Barbara Jean. "Characteristics of Teacher Participation in Curriculum Planning Activities and Reported Acts of Curriculum Implementation." Doctoral dissertation, Northwestern University, Evanston, Illinois, 1969.

King, Arthur R. and John A. Brownell. *The Curriculum and the Disciplines of Knowledge*. New York: John Wiley and Sons, 1966.

Kliebard, Herbert M. "The Tyler Rationale," *The School Review*, 68:259-272, February, 1970.

Kirst, Michael W. and Decker F. Walker. "An Analysis of Curriculum Policy-Making," *Review of Educational Research*, 41:479-509, December, 1971.

Krug, Edward A. *Curriculum Planning*. Rev. ed. New York: Harper and Row, Inc., 1975.

Langenbach, Michael. "The Development of an Instrument to Measure Teachers' Attitudes Toward Curriculum Use and Planning." Doctoral dissertation, Northwestern University, Evanston, Illinois, 1969.

Lundgren, Ulf P. *Frame Factors and the Teaching Process*. Stockholm, Sweden: Almqvist and Wiksell, 1972.

Macdonald, James B., Bernice J. Wolfson, and Esther Zaret. *Reschooling Society: A Conceptual Model.* Washington, D. C.: Association for Supervision and Curriculum Development, 1973.

McNally, Harold J., A. Harry Passow, and Associates. *Improving the Quality of Public School Programs.* New York: Bureau of Publications, Teachers College, Columbia University, 1960.

Neagley, Ross L. and N. Dean Evans. *Handbook for Effective Curriculum Development.* Englewood Cliffs, N.J.: Prentice-Hall, Inc., 1967.

Oliver, Albert I. *Curriculum Improvement.* New York: Dodd, Mead and Company, 1965.

Palardy, J. Michael (ed.). *Elementary School Curriculum: An Anthology of Trends and Challenges.* New York: The Macmillan Company, 1971.

Passow, A. Harry (ed.). *Curriculum Crossroads.* New York: Bureau of Publications, Teachers College, Columbia University, 1962.

Payne, David A. (ed.). *Curriculum Evaluation.* Lexington, Mass.: D. C. Heath and Co., 1974.

Poll, Diana. "A Study of Selected Factors Related to the Implementation of Centrally Prepared Curriculum Guides." Doctoral dissertation, Northwestern University, Evanston, Illinois, 1970.

Ragan, William B. and G. D. Shepherd. *Modern Elementary Curriculum.* 4th ed. New York: Holt, Rinehart and Winston, Inc., 1971.

Robinsohn, Saul B. "A Conceptual Structure of Curriculum Development," *Comparative Education,* 5:221-234, December, 1969.

Saylor, J. Galen and William M. Alexander. *Planning Curriculum for Schools.* New York: Holt, Rinehart and Winston, Inc., 1974.

Smith, B. Othanel, William O. Stanley, and J. Harlan Shores. *Fundamentals of Curriculum Development.* Rev. ed. Yonkers-on-Hudson: World Book Company, 1957.

Sowards, G. Wesley and Mary-Margaret Scobey. *The Changing Curriculum and the Elementary Teacher.* 2d ed. San Francisco: Wadsworth Publishing Company, Inc., 1968.

Stratemeyer, Florence and others. *Developing A Curriculum for Modern Living.* Rev. ed. New York: Bureau of Publications, Teachers College, Columbia University, 1957.

Taba, Hilda. *Curriculum Development: Theory and Practice.* New York: Harcourt, Brace and World, Inc., 1962.

Trump, J. Lloyd and Delmas F. Miller. *Secondary School Curriculum Improvement.* Rockleigh, N. J.: Allyn and Bacon, Inc., 1973.

Tyler, Ralph W. *Basic Principles of Curriculum and Instruction.* Chicago: University of Chicago Press, 1950.

Westbury, Ian. "Curriculum Evaluation," *Review of Educational Research,* 40:239-260, April, 1970.

White, J. P. "The Concept of Curriculum Evaluation," *Journal of Curriculum Studies,* 3:101-112, November, 1971.

Chapter 8

CURRICULUM AS A FIELD OF STUDY

Curriculum as a field of study is a third way the term *curriculum* is used. Curriculum study may include curriculum design, curriculum engineering, curriculum evaluation, curriculum theory and research, foundational backgrounds, and cognitive disciplines. Curriculum as a field of study is one customarily engaged in by graduate students and instructional personnel at colleges and universities. On a less concentrated basis, participants in inservice curriculum programs in schools during the time of their involvement belong in this category.

As we have stated or implied a number of times previously, the field of curriculum is a morass of undefined concepts used without careful definition by many. And when basic concepts are not selected and defined carefully, the boundaries between curriculum and other components of education become blurred. This is true particularly with respect to the boundaries and relationships among curriculum, instruction, evaluation, and learning. Distinctions made in earlier chapters emphasized the need for identifying unique properties and functions. There are many, however, who reject the idea that distinctions should be made among curriculum, instruction, evaluation, and learning. There also are differences in opinion about the domain of a curriculum. We refer here to the use of a single subject, or a discipline, as *curriculum,* such as mathematics curriculum, versus the use of *curriculum* as a referent to the entire program of a school.

In this kind of situation, certain of the theoretical issues in the field can best be noted by an analysis of the conditions and circumstances within the field as revealed in curriculum literature.

CURRICULUM TEXTBOOKS AND COURSES

One way of appraising the field of curriculum is to examine treatments of the field given in textbooks written on curriculum. One type is a wide-coverage book dealing primarily with curriculum development but including chapters on curriculum foundations, curriculum content, and curriculum design. A significant portion of this type of book is devoted to the topics treated in the previous chapter on curriculum engineering.

Another type is the curriculum book that discusses the content and organization of school subjects. These may also have one or more chapters devoted to curriculum planning.

A third type is one in which topics are treated as though curriculum and instruction should be regarded as a common domain. These customarily contain discussions of content, materials of instruction, and modes of teaching for each of the school subjects. Textbooks such as these often contain discussions of administrative organization including nongradedness, tracking, team teaching, and a brief discussion of planning.

Many curriculum books vary from these types by combining elements of each and by diverse treatments of fundamental curriculum concepts. Books of readings in curriculum contain the greatest mixtures of all.

When publishers produce textbooks on curriculum, they do so in the belief that they will be used in college and university courses, and they generally are. The implication here is that courses must vary as much in purpose and content as the textbooks do. Altman analyzed the positions taken by authors on curriculum planning.[1] He developed a model for classifying treatments of objectives in curriculum planning and the activities recommended for achieving those objectives. Altman found great differences in both objectives and activities for curriculum planning in the various positions. Content variation in curriculum planning books is an indication that similar variation takes place in courses devoted to curriculum development.

Range and variation in curriculum course offerings is another indication of the confusion that reigns in the field of curriculum.

---

[1] Burton E. Altman, "An Identification and Classification of Selected Characteristics of Cooperative Curriculum Planning Positions from 1918 to 1965" (Doctoral dissertation, Northwestern University, Evanston, Illinois, 1965).

The condition of course offerings in curriculum is typified by a study of Bateman.[2] He surveyed the course offerings in elementary curriculum offered by universities having undergraduate programs in elementary teacher education. The results of the study dramatically pointed out that content variation is a characteristic of such courses. In elementary teacher education, the courses tend to cover the whole gamut of elementary education.

Wootton also surveyed curriculum offerings in teacher education institutions.[3] He reported many observations similar to those of Bateman. Wootton, however, was more convinced than Bateman that the language of curriculum is being refined. Later, Wootton and Selwa noted increased difficulty in identifying any body of content to which every student of curriculum should be exposed.[4] Then in a third survey, Wootton, Reynolds, and Lopp found offerings in the curriculum field to be significantly expanded.[5] Further, changes in the nature of offerings were noted by the authors. Their 1973 survey revealed a more even distribution among several categories like elementary and secondary curriculum and curriculum development indicating that more attention is being given to various aspects of curriculum. It is noteworthy that 6% of the courses offered in 1973 were studies in "Curriculum Research and Evaluation;" whereas, in the original survey there were no such courses. Content offered in courses showed a significant increase in field-centered experiences and "problem solving." Results also indicated that a broader population is being reached by institutions having curriculum courses; the percentage of courses open to teachers, administrators, curriculum directors, and supervisors jumped from 29% in 1969 to 71% in 1973, and those open to college professors jumped from 1% to 39%. However, it appears that institutions confuse curriculum and method in identifying courses since 75 courses

---

[2]Donald G. Bateman, "An Investigation of the Circumstances and Conditions of the Undergraduate Course in Elementary School Curriculum in Teacher Education Programs in Selected Universities in the United States" (Doctoral dissertation, Northwestern University, Evanston, Illinois, 1966).

[3]Lutian R. Wootton, "The Curriculum: Is the Concept Changing?" *Clearing House*, 42:143-145, November, 1967.

[4]Lutian R. Wootton and Robert W. Selwa, "Curriculum: A Changing Concept," *Educational Leadership*, 27:692-696, April, 1970.

[5]Lutian R. Wootton, John C. Reynolds, Jr., and Jerrell E. Lopp, "Curriculum Content and Experiences: A Comparative Survey," *Educational Leadership*, 31:431-434, February, 1974.

were reported by institutions to be curriculum courses, but only 9 of these were categorized by the researchers as curriculum. It is evident, therefore, that there is still confusion or lack of refinement in curriculum language.

RESEARCH

The journals most concerned with reviewing research in education are the *Review of Educational Research* and the *American Educational Research Journal.* A substantial number of the contributors to the summaries and articles devoted to curriculum have noted the paucity of curriculum research.

An interesting picture of the status of curriculum research is revealed in the 1960, the 1963, the 1966, and the 1969 June issues of the *Review*. The four issues contain twenty-seven chapters. Four of the twenty-seven contain discussions of the state of the field. Five fall under the general heading of forces influencing curriculum decisions. Two are devoted to curriculum components or design. Two chapters highlight teaching. Three review curriculum development processes. The conditions of curriculum theory and research are the topics of five. And four of the twenty-seven chapters are devoted to materials and media. One of the four issues contains five chapters, another ten chapters, and two six chapters, but this does not mean that topics treated in the ten-chapter issue were not treated more briefly somewhere in the other two. Many were. Nevertheless, this analysis of chapters gives some picture of the concerns of persons interested in curriculum research.

Goodlad concluded in 1960 that: "Curriculum theorizing to date is best described as abstract speculation; curriculum research as 'Dust-bowl' empiricism; and curriculum practice as rule-of-thumb guesswork. . . ."[6] To this Abramson added the following in 1966:

> The curriculum field has been very rich in statements of philosophy and principles, but, . . . is lacking in theoretical formulations which engender researchable hypotheses. Because of both the attempt to conduct research on the basis of the holistic view of curriculum and the derivative nature of its methodology, curriculum research has been

---

[6]John I. Goodlad, "Curriculum: The State of the Field," *Review of Educational Research*, 30:195, June, 1960.

based predominantly on pupil testing, as has research in teaching and instruction.[7]

Abramson raises here the question of criteria for evaluation of curriculums and curriculum practices. Macdonald challenged the use of pupil learning as a criterion for curriculum evaluation. He suggested that once a curriculum is the output of a curriculum system, it would be more appropriate to use such criteria as degree of use of the curriculum made by teachers, teacher attitudes toward the curriculum, and so forth.[8] Goodlad summarized the 1969 issue. One of his conclusions was that "General theory and conceptualization in curriculum appear to have advanced very little during the last decade."[9]

In a provocative paper on curriculum research, Walker examined the following thesis:

> We in the field of curriculum have failed to conduct the empirical research needed to clarify the nature of the phenomena and problems we address. This failure is due in large part to misconceptions we have uncritically accepted of the nature and aims of empirical inquiry in a field concerned with practice, and, as a result of these misconceptions, our lack of faith in empirical inquiry as a means of dealing with our concerns.[10]

He defined as the central problem of curriculum that which should be taught, studied, or learned. Walker warned of traps involved in borrowing inappropriate rules for research patterns from the behavioral sciences, and he suggested instead that we should find more appropriate ways of getting factual information by observing and manipulating curriculum phenomena to help formulate and resolve curriculum problems.

It is apparent from reviews of research on curriculum that the research effort has not been making major contributions to the definition of curriculum as a field. The basic problems of scientific theorizing in curriculum have not been faced, or resolved, by

---

[7]David A. Abramson, "Curriculum Research and Evaluation," *Review of Educational Research*, 36:389, June, 1966.

[8]James B. Macdonald, "Curriculum Theory: Problems and A Prospectus" (a mimeographed paper presented at the meeting of Professors of Curriculum, Miami Beach, 1964).

[9]John I. Goodlad, "Curriculum: State of the Field," *Review of Educational Research*, 39:374, June, 1969.

[10]Decker Walker, "What Curriculum Research?" (A mimeographed paper presented at the Annual Convention of the American Educational Research Association, Chicago, Illinois, April 4, 1972), p. 1.

curriculum researchers, too few of whom are specialists in curriculum theory.

COMMON DENOMINATORS

Despite the great diversity of opinion about curriculum as a field of study, as reflected by the discussion of the previous sections of this chapter, there do appear to be some common denominators to which all seriously thinking persons in curriculum, particularly theorists, must and do pay attention. As curriculum theorists identify and characterize both the common and uncommon denominators of curriculum as a field of study, they will be led to more sophisticated and to more sharply differentiated theories. In the following paragraphs, some basic and common dimensions of curriculum as a field of study are indicated with the caution that diverse opinions may exist within them.

Curriculum Design and Engineering

First among these common denominators are those that have been discussed in previous chapters under the titles of Curriculum Design and Curriculum Engineering. There is no need for us to review here the previous discussions about these components of the curriculum field. Few, if any, would deny that the problems and issues of curriculum design and the organization of culture content belong in the domain of curriculum, but conversely, many would disagree about specific dimensions of those problems and issues. Similarly, we can recognize curriculum engineering as an established component of the field of curriculum. Certainly, a curriculum must be planned if it is to exist. Once a curriculum exists people need to implement it. Avowedly, it should be revised continuously, and revision demands evaluation. Although diverse curriculum practices do reflect different curriculum positions, they nevertheless belong within the field of curriculum.

We may consider curriculum design and curriculum engineering to be the essential components of the field of curriculum, but they must be supported by research and theory building in order to qualify as a field of study. Even though there may be a paucity of both research and theory-building efforts within the field of curriculum, substantial future progress as a field of study is dependent upon them.

Curriculum Experience

Our past experience in curriculum affairs is another facet of curriculum that students may share. Probably a substantial share of graduate study in the field of curriculum is a matter of reviewing the past experience by consulting works that have been written in both the immediate and remote past. Procedurally, a student of curriculum may wish to explore experience in curriculum matters from three perspectives: reports of curriculum programs in school systems, analysis of positions taken by curriculum writers, and attacks upon the field of curriculum as a whole in historical perspective. We have some examples from each of these in the literature. For example, the book entitled *Curriculum Improvement in Public School Systems* published by Hollis Caswell and associates in 1950 reported nine current curriculum programs.[11] A decade later, McNally, Passow, and associates published a sequel to Caswell's report.[12] They reported on curriculum practices in seven state, county, or district communities. Future scholars would provide increased clarity to the practical dimensions of curriculum design and engineering if more reporting of this type were done.

Various writers in curriculum have recorded and published their positions on curriculum matters. These do exist, and they are a matter of common record for students of the curriculum field. A weakness of the field is that these contrasting positions are not openly and vigorously debated. It appears as if curriculum scholars fear that they may hurt one another's feelings. We have not had a definitive work in which curriculum postures were frankly and openly discussed since the two-part Twenty-sixth Yearbook of the National Society for the Study of Education under the chairmanship of Harold Rugg was published in 1927. Furthermore, researchers seldom focus upon critical and comparative analysis of organized curriculum postures. Altman's

---

[11]Hollis L. Caswell and associates, *Curriculum Improvement in Public School Systems*, (New York: Bureau of Publications, Teachers College, Columbia University, 1950).

[12]Harold J. McNally, A. Harry Passow, and associates, *Improving the Quality of Public School Programs* (New York: Bureau of Publications, Teachers College, Columbia University, 1960).

study[13] of positions on curriculum planning was unique in this respect. Seguel's analysis of the curriculum works of the McMurrys, John Dewey, Franklin Bobbitt, Harold Rugg, and Hollis Caswell is a very singular work.[14] Critical and comparative analysis of published works is a very rich and profitable area for concentration of research effort.

Another way in which our past experience is a common denominator to the field of curriculum is the development of the field in historical perspective. This dimension is reflected through the ebb and flow of postures taken by curriculum scholars, research trends, and vagaries in curriculum practices in schools. When it was the policy of the American Educational Research Association to publish an issue of the *Review of Educational Research* on curriculum once every three years, historical studies reflecting such attention to the past dimensions of the field were occasionally reviewed. For example, in the June of 1957 issue Beauchamp prepared a chapter entitled "Curriculum Organization and Development in Historical Perspective."[15] Similarly in the June of 1969 issue Bellack prepared a chapter entitled "History of Curriculum Thought and Practice."[16]

Two studies conducted by individuals serve as exemplars of needed research on the development of the field. One is the study by Phillips[17] in which he traced how the concept "curriculum" had been used since Bobbitt wrote the first definitive work on curriculum in 1918. The study by Seguel[18] was broader in scope as she reviewed the development of curriculum as a field during its formative years by using the work of individuals as illustrative of various periods or stages of development. A sequel to this carefully executed study is much needed, and there is a study covering the period between 1940 and 1973 currently being developed by Gregory Mullen at Northwestern University.

---

[13]*Op. cit.*

[14]Mary Louise Seguel, *The Curriculum Field: Its Formative Years* (New York: Teachers College Press, Teachers College, Columbia University, 1966).

[15]George A. Beauchamp, "Curriculum Organization and Development in Historical Perspective," *Review of Educational Research*, 27:239-261, June, 1957.

[16]Arno A. Bellack, "History of Curriculum Thought and Practice," *Review of Educational Research*, 39:283-292, June, 1969.

[17]Richard C. Phillips, "A Historical Study of the Concept Curriculum" (Doctoral dissertation, Northwestern University, Evanston, Illinois, 1962).

[18]*Op. cit.*

Organized Fields of Knowledge

Certain organized fields of knowledge constitute another rough common denominator of the field of curriculum. Particularly identifiable are the so-called educational foundations, the parent disciplines to the culture content of school subjects, and the disciplines that are cognate to the study of curriculum.

Few students of the field of curriculum would deny the need to include the study of educational foundations as part of the field of curriculum. This is evidenced by the fact that most authors of textbooks on curriculum include chapters covering such subjects as the history of curriculum efforts, principles of learning, human growth and development, cultural and social information about schools including political forces, and tenets from the philosophy of education. These subjects have been treated as the foundations of education in general with scholars in each specific component of education, including curriculum, drawing from them information and authority for much of their work. The significance of foundational influences upon education is highlighted by positions occupied by people in professional education. Each foundational area has a parent in the conventional discipline — educational psychology has one in psychology, philosophy of education in philosophy, educational sociology in sociology, and so forth. But education is an applied discipline, and it is the job of the educational psychologist, the philosopher of education, and the sociologist to apply knowledge from their parent disciplines to education. The same is true for students of the field of curriculum. They must study the import of knowledge from related disciplines for the characteristics and functions of curriculum.

The parent disciplines of the culture content to be used as school subject matter are another common denominator for the field of curriculum. The organized fields of knowledge are constantly changing their configurations, and where appropriate, school curricula should reflect such changes. For example, if historians through their research efforts come up with valid and reliable reinterpretations of American colonial history, those interpretations should be reflected in social studies programs for both elementary and secondary schools. Dozens of similar specified content illustrations could be given from other disciplines. Additionally, new rationales for the organization of school subjects are proposed within the parent disciplines, and these rationales must be prerequisite information for selecting and organizing culture content for a school's curriculum. All of which points to the organized disciplines as a necessary and common dimension of curriculum as a field of study, and the focal point for such knowledge in curriculum design.

A third common denominator for students of curriculum consists of those disciplines that are cognate to the field of curriculum, particularly that portion having to do with curriculum engineering. I contend that too many of those who write about curriculum theory ignore both the substance of curriculum engineering and the source disciplines for leadership behaviors in the processes of curriculum engineering. The exploration of philosophy of science, logic, organizational behavior theory, political science, and sociology are vivid examples of studies that are highly desirable, if not essential, for anyone who wishes to become a student of the complete field of curriculum. The study of learning theory and epistemology are two additional fields of study that are useful to the curriculum specialist but more appropriately related to curriculum design. To these may be added statistics, research design, and computer technology as source disciplines to the research and theory-building component of the curriculum field. It is from the cognate disciplines that the curriculum theorist searches for paradigms for his own theory-building activities. The ability to make such translations is one of the curriculum specialist's more important skills.

Thus, curriculum design and curriculum engineering are fundamental components of the field of curriculum in the sense that these components are what the field is all about. When you add research on design, engineering, and theory development to them, you will have circumscribed the dimensions of the field of study. However, the basic dimensions of the field are not enough to adequately describe all of what actually are the common denominators of the field. Curriculum is an applied discipline, at least an applied area of study. As such, it not only develops its own history in the form of experience with design, engineering, research, and theory; it furthers its development through the constant reapplication of knowledge from foundational areas and related disciplines.

SUMMARY AND A POINT OF VIEW

When interpretations of the field of curriculum are guided principally by the search for answers to questions about what shall be taught in a school, it is easier to identify commonality among those interpretations than when interpretations of the field of curriculum are guided by search for answers to questions about what shall be taught in schools *and* to questions about how to teach whatever is to be taught. When theories and research are inadequate to explain and support those interpretations, the state of the field appears chaotic and ill-defined. The discussion presented in this chapter supports these generalizations.

Careful scrutiny of literature does indicate that there is substantial agreement that certain large areas belong under the umbrella of the curriculum field. In this chapter, I have identified curriculum content and design, curriculum engineering, research and theory development, and the study of related disciplines as common dimensions of curriculum as a field of study. Despite nominal agreement about the inclusion of these large areas within the field, writers show considerable disparity in meanings associated with fundamental concepts in curriculum. Chief among these are definitions of a curriculum, conceived uses for a curriculum, and the processes of curriculum development.

The work of curriculum theorists is an encouraging phenomenon. Theorists have the opportunity to capitalize upon the common and uncommon denominators of the present status of the curriculum field by using them as springboards for better and unique theories. In the process, curriculum as a field of study should become more clarified.

My point of view on the substance of curriculum as a field of study already has been exhibited in the summaries of the chapters on curriculum design and curriculum engineering and in the section of this chapter dealing with common denominators of the field. For me, the essential ingredients of the curriculum field are nested in deliberations about curriculum content and design and about the processes of curriculum engineering. For curriculum to be recognized as a field of scholarship, research and theory development covering the broad spectra of design and engineering are essential. The primary assumption behind these statements is that the question of what shall be taught in a school is the singular problem of the field of curriculum. Questions about how to teach belong in the broad field of education, but they should be included in the field of instruction.

SUGGESTED READINGS

Note: Most of the suggested readings at the end of Chapter 7 also are relevant here.

Altman, Burton E. "An Identification and Classification of Selected Characteristics of Cooperative Curriculum Planning Positions from 1918 to 1965." Doctoral dissertation, Northwestern University, Evanston, Illinois, 1965.

Association for Supervision and Curriculum Development, NEA. *Research for Curriculum Improvement.* 1957 Yearbook. Washington, D.C.: the Association, 1957.

Bateman, Donald G. "An Investigation of the Circumstances and Conditions of the Undergraduate Course in Elementary School Curriculum in Teacher Education Programs in Selected Universities in the United States." Doctoral dissertation, Northwestern University, Evanston, Illinois, 1966.

Eisner, Elliot W. (ed.). *Confronting Curriculum Reform.* Boston: Little, Brown and Company, 1971.

Huebner, Dwayne (ed.). *A Reassessment of the Curriculum.* New York: Bureau of Publications, Teachers College, Columbia University, 1964.

Kerr, J. F. *The Problem of Curriculum Reform.* Leicester, England: Leicester University Press, 1967.

Kliebard, Herbert. "The Curriculum Field in Retrospect," *Technology and the Curriculum.* P. W. F. Witt (ed.). New York: Teachers College Press, 1968. pp. 69-84.

McClure, Robert M. (ed.). *The Curriculum: Restrospect and Prospect.* The Seventieth Yearbook of the National Society for the Study of Education. Chicago: The University of Chicago Press, 1971.

Parker, J. Cecil and Louis J. Rubin. *Process as Content: Curriculum Design and the Application of Knowledge.* Chicago: Rand McNally and Company, 1966.

Phillips, Richard Claybourne. "An Historical Study of the Concept Curriculum." Doctoral dissertation, Northwestern University, Evanston, Illinois, 1962.

Robinson, Helen R. (ed.). *Precedents and Promise in the Curriculum Field.* New York: Teachers College Press, Teachers College, Columbia University, 1966.

Seguel, Mary Louise. *The Curriculum Field: Its Formative Years.* New York: Teachers College Press, Teachers College, Columbia University, 1966.

Short, Edmund C. (ed.). "A Search for Valid Content for Curriculum Courses," *Educational Comment/1970*. Toledo, Ohio: College of Education, University of Toledo, 1970.

Short, Edmund C. "Knowledge Production and Utilization in Curriculum: A Special Case of the General Phenomenon," *Review of Educational Research,* 43:237-302, Summer, 1973.

Smith, B. Othanel and Robert H. Ennis. *Language and Concepts in Education.* Chicago: Rand McNally and Company, 1961.

Tyler, Louise L. *A Selected Guide to Curriculum Literature: An Annotated Bibliography.* Washington: National Educational Association, 1970.

Venable, Tom C. *Philosophical Foundations of the Curriculum.* Chicago: Rand McNally and Company, 1967.

Wootton, Lutian R. "The Curriculum: Is the Concept Changing," *Clearing House,* 42:143-145, November, 1967.

Wootton, Lutian R. and Robert W. Selwa. "Curriculum: A Changing Concept," *Educational Leadership*, 27:692-696, April, 1970.

Chapter 9

THE NUCLEUS OF A CURRICULUM THEORY

The first two editions of this book were criticized, in part, because, in the judgment of the critics, I had failed to state a curriculum theory in full or that I had not made it clear what my curriculum theory was. I had thought that I had evidenced these things, but apparently the message did not get communicated well. Hence, in this edition, the final chapter is devoted to a statement of my curriculum theory as it has evolved in my thinking up to this point in time.

This statement of my curriculum theory will be set forth by following some of the admonitions for theorists set forth in Chapter 2. It should already be quite clear to the reader that I consider curriculum as a field to be essentially two dimensional: one part concerned with curriculum design and the other with curriculum engineering. Curriculum as a field of study is concerned with the historical antecedents, and with research and theory-building activity necessary to further explain those two dimensions. Within each of these dimensions, I shall begin by setting forth the definitions of key terms that are essential to one's understanding of the theory. The definitions will be followed by a set of propositions that I think are warranted either by assumption, by postulate, or by generalization from research literature. A statement will be included beneath each proposition delineating its character.

Basic Definitions

Meanings associated with certain basic terms are crucial to understanding my position on curriculum design and curriculum engineering. These should be clear to the reader by now, but I include them here as reminders since they are so crucial to my position. They include: a curriculum, curriculum design, a curriculum system, curriculum engineering, and curriculum as a field of study.

A curriculum is a written plan depicting the scope and arrangement of the projected educational program for a school. Optimally, the curriculum should contain: (1) a statement of intention for use of the document as a guiding force for planning instructional strategies, (2) statements outlining the goals for the school for which the curriculum was designed, (3) a body of culture content that has the potential for the realization of the goals, and (4) a statement of an evaluation scheme for determining the worth and the effectiveness of the curriculum and the curriculum system.

Curriculum design is the substance and organization of goals and culture content so arranged as to reveal potential progression through levels of schooling.

A curriculum system is a system for decision making and action with respect to the three primary curriculum functions: curriculum planning, curriculum implementation, and curriculum evaluation.

Curriculum engineering consists of all the processes and activities necessary to maintain and improve a curriculum system including leadership by persons occupying such positions as superintendent, principal, and curriculum director.

Curriculum as a field of study refers to the continuous exploration of curriculum design, curriculum engineering, their historical antecedents, and the necessary research and theory building to further explain them.

CURRICULUM DESIGN

Curriculum design was defined above as the substance and organization of goals and culture content so arranged as to reveal potential progression for learners through levels of schooling. So used, the word *design* is a noun rather than a verb form, and consequently, the language used to describe design must be focused upon an object — the curriculum. By choosing to use only the noun form, I must assign the verb form *designing* to the processes of curriculum planning. This means that curriculum planning groups must select, or create, a design for the curriculum they plan.

Design Definitions

The key term for curriculum design is *a curriculum.* Since it was defined above, it need not be repeated here, but all of the following definitions expand upon the concept of a curriculum.

Curriculum contents refer to all of the components of a curriculum. The term is used here in much the same sense that a table of contents is used to depict the chapters of a book.

Goals are those statements within a curriculum that indicate the ends toward which the school is to strive.

Culture content is that portion of man's total knowledge that is selected to be used in the school as a means of achieving the goals that have been set forth. Culture content may be classified in three categories. *Cognitive culture content* consists of the substantive elements of our culture reflected through key concepts and generalizations derived from man's accumulated knowledge. *Affective culture content* consists of those elements of our culture that are value-oriented. *Inquiry and skill culture content* consists of those processes and ways of behaving essential for communication and for conducting inquiry into problems of the culture. The syntactics associated with the basic disciplines are included here.

Subjects are simply ways of organizing culture content into homogenous realms for teaching purposes. Mathematics, social studies, language arts, science, music may be spoken of as subjects.

Disciplines are basic branches of knowledge that are organized to facilitate their instruction and their development. Physics, history, philosophy, mathematics, anthropology are examples.

Processes is a general term for inquiry processes, syntactics, skill behaviors, and other learning processes. Herein, they are treated as culture content in equal status with cognitive and affective culture content.

Fusion is a process of reducing the number of realms of culture content to be included in a curriculum by integrating two or more extant realms. Frequently cited results of fusion are the social studies, the language arts, persistent life situations, molar problems, and the core curriculum.

The term *scope* is used to refer to the magnitude of goals and culture content in a curriculum. Magnitude may be thought of as breadth at various levels for which curriculum entries are pertinent as well as the breadth of the entire curriculum for a school.

The term *sequence* is used to speak of the ordinal arrangement of the culture content elements in a curriculum. The more severe consideration in sequence occurs when certain culture content is prerequisite for others. Therefore, sequential or ordinal arrangement is important within and between levels for which the curriculum is designed as well as for the entire school.

Articulation is a process of relating the realms of culture content within and among the various levels of school organization. Articulation is necessary both vertically and horizontally within that organization.

Levels of organization refers to the manner in which pupils are organized for purposes of instruction. Conventionally, these levels have been grades. In a non-graded situation, the levels may have other names.

Rationale refers to the explanation for the organization of any given realm of culture content. If a realm of culture content is social studies, the rationale is the explanation for the selection and distribution of its elements. If a realm is to be identified as molar problems, the rationale must explain the selection and scope of those problems.

Design Propositions

In addition to definitional statements, my theory of curriculum design can be expanded by the formulation of propositions. In Chapter 2, a proposition was described as a formal statement affirming or denying something about a subject. Such statements as postulates, generalizations, and hypotheses were indicated to be special cases of the proposition. By way of organization, I shall first indicate my propositions, and beneath each statement, a further explanation of it and an indication of the degree of confidence in which I hold it will be added. This is necessary since some of the propositions are assumptive or prescriptive statements; whereas, others approach the level of firm generalizations.

Proposition # 1

A curriculum is a written document.

A curriculum must be a written document in order for maximum use to be made of it. A curriculum is a conceptualized plan for the total educational program of the school. As such, it becomes the central force for the development of instructional strategies by all teachers who teach in the school. A curriculum should be constantly under appraisal and revision. It must be written to be so used and treated.

Proposition #2

> The major purpose for having a curriculum is to establish a basic environmental structure from which teachers will develop teaching strategies for specific classroom groups.

The essence of the basic environmental structure is reflected in the form and arrangement of curriculum design. Teachers will provide for learning opportunities and instructional materials in their instructional strategies. The basic environmental structure described in the curriculum provides a holistic base for all instruction.

Proposition #3

> To be most effective as an instrument for directing instruction, a curriculum should optimally consist of four parts: (1) a set of directions for teachers about the use of the curriculum within the curriculum system, (2) a listing of the educational goals for the school, (3) a body of culture content selected in the anticipation that the culture content will be instrumental in the achievement of the designated goals, and (4) a scheme for the evaluation and revision of the curriculum.

This proposition presents what I consider to be the optimal ingredients of a curriculum. They were illustrated in Figure 9, page 129, and the parts were described in the accompanying discussion. There should be no need for further explication here other than to emphasize the dynamics of the design. Goals are selected. Realms of culture content believed to be useful in the achievement of the goals are selected and organized. The curriculum is used as intended. The curriculum is evaluated, thus providing data for revision of the several parts. Revision data cause the goals, the culture content, and the use of the curriculum to be reconsidered. In this way, a dynamic cycle of curriculum analysis is invoked.

Proposition #4

> *A curriculum should contain four categories of goals: cognitive, syntactical, affective, and applicative.*

The statement of educational goals in a curriculum must be sufficiently broad to encompass the full range of the intended educational program. It assumes that any educational program would anticipate cognitive, syntactical, affective, and applicative learnings. Cognitive goals would refer to the basic concepts of knowledge, key ideas, generalizations, principles, and laws. Syntactical goals would refer to modes of inquiry for solving problems in the areas of organized knowledge such as observation, classification, inference, prediction, as well as the psychomotor skills of communication and expression. Affective goals would refer to those values, beliefs, emotions, attitudes, and appreciations deemed important for inclusion in the curriculum. Applicative goals would refer to those aspirations for learnings associated with social and personal problems of living, particularly problems demanding that knowledge and skills developed in the first three categories be applied.

Proposition #5

> *The culture content of a curriculum is selected and organized because that culture content is believed to be most useful for teachers to use in achieving the stated goals.*

Our culture content has become so massive that, to a very great extent, the process of curriculum planning is one of selecting from the total mass. The governing criteria for selection are the evolving purposes of schools. We should never forget that the increasing tempo of generating knowledge, coupled with the constantly changing social environment, demands consistent evaluation and subsequent modification of our response to the question of what should the schools teach. Furthermore, the selection of culture content for the curriculum is a much too important decision to be left to the whimsies of individual teachers at the level of planning instructional strategies. Curriculum planners are obligated to conceptualize the educational program for a school by determining goals and devising an organized body of culture content they believe will be useful in the attainment of the goals.

Proposition #6

Goals, or objectives, and related culture content for schools are political decisions. Curriculum planners must verify those they use through political channels.

The policy making agency for any school district is the Board of Education. Curricula for the schools under the jurisdiction of the Board of Education are fundamental policy of the district. Therefore, the agency for screening and approval of all curriculum decisions is the school board. Likewise in every educational institution other than public elementary and secondary schools, there will be some policy-making group bearing responsibility similar to the school board for the curriculum for that institution. This proposition is axiomatic for all decisions relative to the contents of a curriculum.

Proposition #7

Culture content in a curriculum may be organized in terms of realms, components, and levels of organization.

The culture content of a curriculum is described in a variety of ways. Sometimes culture content elements are spoken of as subject matter; at other times they are referred to as fused components of the various disciplines; but perhaps the most commonly used term is school subjects. I have used the term culture content to refer to any and all of these designations that may be chosen as a basis for organization of knowledge that is intended to be used with school students in response to stipulated goals. The realms of culture content may be stipulated in terms of conventional disciplines, fused disciplines that have been brought together, molar problems, or any other way of designating the nature of the various culture content packages that may be used. Curriculum planners may also wish to indicate in their design the cognitive, affective, and inquiry or skill components that are expected to emerge from exposure to the realms of culture content. Both the realms of culture content and the components of culture content should be organized to fit the organizational pattern of a school.

Proposition #8

The rationale for the form and arrangement of the realms of culture content in a curriculum must be reflected in the curriculum design.

Each of the realms of culture content in a curriculum should have a rationale, or an explanation, for its form and arrangement. There are so many different possibilities for the selection and arrangement of culture content that curriculum planners should make clear what it is they have selected and how they have organized it. Scope and sequence arrangements are but part of the explanation. Each of the realms of culture content may have different rationales and not in any way jeopardize the overall intent of the curriculum planners.

Proposition #9

The younger the learners for whom the curriculum is designed the more fused the culture content should be.

This proposition is an assumption on my part. It seems to me that for the younger children in school, learning can be more efficient and useful in a wider variety of situations if the number of subjects is reduced and the interrelationships among various culture content ingredients are reflected through their applications in more common domains. The younger the minds of the learners, the less adept they are at making transitions from highly and individually organized separate subjects or disciplines.

Proposition #10

For students in the secondary school, the culture content should be organized by a combination of established disciplines in the sciences, the social sciences, and the humanities, units devoted to molar problems, and specialized vocational content.

The reasons for this proposition should be self-evident. The greater maturity of the secondary school student will allow him to study in the individual disciplines and to make certain transitions between or among them on his own power. In addition, secondary schools of America cannot ignore teaching about molar problems and their potential solutions as well as more specialized vocational content. The balance to be maintained among these is greatly dependent upon where the secondary school students go and what they do when they leave the secondary school.

Proposition #11

> *The design of a curriculum and the organizational pattern of the school need to be in harmony in order to facilitate the implementation of the curriculum.*

The relationship here should be clear. It is one thing to create a curriculum design to fit a graded type school. It is quite another to plan a curriculum that will fit some version of a non-graded school. What needs to be kept in mind is that the curriculum should be a useful tool to teachers for purposes of developing their teaching strategies. If their teaching strategies are going to be applied to students organized in a graded manner, teachers have one kind of a problem. They have another if the school is organized in various levels of non-graded structure. It simply makes sense that the organizational pattern of the school and the organizational pattern expressed in curriculum design should be in harmony.

Proposition #12

> *The choice of culture content can be made independently of instructional methods, but the choice of instructional method is dependent upon the nature of the culture content.*

I set forth this proposition to offset the argument that methodological considerations need to be included in curriculum design. The methods of teaching are greatly dependent upon the nature of the content to be taught. We have known and recognized this for a long time. On the other hand, the choice of culture content in a curriculum is in response to the goals. And the choice of that culture content can be made independently of instructional methods that may follow. It must be said that curriculum planners may anticipate in general the nature of instructional method, but the inclusion of a prescription of method is not a part of curriculum design.

CURRICULUM ENGINEERING

In the basic definitions set forth at the beginning of this chapter, curriculum engineering was defined to consist of all of the processes and activities necessary to maintain and improve a curriculum system including leadership by persons occupying such positions as superintendent, principal, and curriculum director.

The curriculum engineering processes are applied to the curriculum system which has been defined as a system for decision making and action with respect to the three primary curriculum functions: curriculum planning, curriculum implementation, and curriculum evaluation. In this section, I will proceed in the same way that I did in the section on curriculum design by establishing particular definitions appropriate to curriculum engineering and follow those with a series of propositions that are particularly appropriate for curriculum engineering as I see them at the present time.

Engineering Definitions

Curriculum planning consists of all the processes necessary to plan for and to write a curriculum. The processes include the choosing of an arena for the curriculum planning, the selection and organization of personnel to do the planning, the execution of working procedures necessary to relate input information to the curriculum decisions resulting in the curriculum itself.

Curriculum implementation refers to those processes necessary to insure that the curriculum is used by teachers as a point of departure for the development of their teaching strategies.

Curriculum evaluation consists of those processes necessary to judge the effectiveness of the curriculum that was planned as well as the effectiveness of the curriculum system itself.

Arena is the term I use to describe the geographic-social environment in which curriculum planning, curriculum implementation, and/or curriculum evaluation is undertaken. The most common choices available to a theorist as potential arenas for curriculum planning, implementation, and evaluation are the nation, the state, the school district, or the individual school. The arena for curriculum planning may be different from the arena for curriculum implementation, and both may be different from the arena for curriculum evaluation. When such is the case, we can say that the arena is split among the curriculum functions.

Involvement refers to the selection and utilization of persons who are to do curriculum planning, curriculum implementation, and/or curriculum evaluation.

Input consists of the knowledge and human resources necessary to the curriculum planning processes.

Output refers to the output of the curriculum system. The principal output of a curriculum system is a curriculum.

Engineering Propositions

The following propositions are related to the purposes and functions of curriculum engineering. I shall continue the organization used in the treatment of design propositions by first stating each proposition and following it with a brief explication.

Proposition #13

> *The general purpose of a curriculum system as one of the several systems of schooling is to provide a framework for deciding what shall be taught in the schools and to provide for employing those decisions as points of departure for developing instructional strategies.*

This proposition is assumptive and axiomatic to my curriculum theory. My contention is that the primary curriculum question is "What shall be taught in the schools?." The answer to this question should be conceived holistically; that is, it should be conceived in terms of the wholeness of a school or a school district, preferably a school. This is an application of the Gestalt principle that the whole is greater than the sum of all its parts. A curriculum in terms of what shall be taught in a school represents a conception of what the education of the pupils who are to attend that school should be in its totality. Instruction in the individual classrooms within that school for children at various age levels are atomistic parts of the total educational plan carried out within the domain of the instructional system. It is a secondary purpose of a curriculum system to insure that the curriculum decisions are used by teachers for developing unique instructional strategies for children under their jurisdiction using the curriculum as a point of departure.

Proposition #14

> *A distinction must be made between curriculum planning and inputs that may influence decisions at the level of curriculum planning.*

In order to identify and maintain control over curriculum planning efforts within a curriculum system it is necessary to recognize that it is one thing to perform the acts of curriculum planning but that it is quite another to consider those inputs that may influence the decisions of the curriculum planners. Great identity confusion frequently is perpetrated by referring to persons and agencies that may supply useful information to curriculum planners as being part of the curriculum planning effort. The crux of this proposition lies in the assumption that a curriculum is to be planned and that the persons selected from the arena in which the curriculum is to be planned are the curriculum planners. Anyone else, or any idea, is an input, or influence upon the curriculum planning decisions.

Proposition #15

> *Curriculum engineering is markedly facilitated when the arena for planning and implementing are the same.*

This proposition is at the level of a generalization. Research has established that teachers who have participated in curriculum planning are more apt to use the curriculum as a point of departure for developing instructional strategies and to be more willing and enthusiastic to do so. The more removed the arena for curriculum planning is from the arena in which the implementation effort is directed, the less identity teachers feel with the curriculum and the more they resist its implementation.

Proposition #16

> *Curriculum implementation is greatly facilitated when planning groups include classroom teachers who must do the implementing.*

This proposition is a corollary to proposition #2. When the planning group and the implementing group are one and the same, curriculum implementation is greatly facilitated if only through the identification of the classroom teachers with the curriculum as well as their dedication to use it because they feel that curriculum to be the result of their own labors. Again, this proposition is a generalization from existing research.

Proposition #17

> *A reciprocal relationship exists between the selection of people to be involved in curriculum planning and the choice of the arena within which the curriculum is to be utilized.*

The first choice for curriculum engineers is the choice of the arena within which the curriculum is to function. In the United States, the most frequent choices are the school district or the individual school building. More simply, the question is whether the curriculum shall be planned for an entire district or whether the curriculum shall be planned for an individual school. Once the arena choice is made, then discussion can take place about who is to be involved in the curriculum planning. Normally, only persons from the chosen arena will be selected. Those external to that arena would be considered as resource people to the persons who actually are to make the curriculum decisions. On the other hand, it is possible that curriculum engineers may wish to decide upon who shall be involved in curriculum planning prior to the arena choice. In that case, selection and involvement of people in curriculum planning is a top priority consideration in the minds of the curriculum engineers, and the selection may then markedly influence the arena choice.

Proposition #18

> *The re-education of teachers about new and potential curriculum content is better accomplished through teacher participation in curriculum planning than by means used when teachers do not participate in curriculum planning.*

Planning groups are greatly affected by the exchange of ideas with one another in the planning process. Planning groups are exposed to information that others normally are not, and the input information is specifically pointed to that school's efforts. The general type of in-service workshop is less adequate for the re-education of teachers if one only considers the longevity of those workshops in comparison with the practice of continuous curriculum planning and revision over a long period of time.

Proposition #19

> *The more removed the curriculum planning function is from classroom teachers, the more restrictive the curriculum is upon the professional judgment of teachers.*

A curriculum that is planned remotely from the classroom teacher who must implement it is considered by the teacher who implements it to be a mandate from elsewhere. The teacher is less familiar with the content and implication of the curriculum. Both of these considerations contribute to the rejection of the curriculum as a point of departure for the development of teaching strategies and to the use of unimaginative teaching strategies. A remotely planned curriculum tends to make a follower of the classroom teacher rather than a creative professional person, but when a curriculum has been planned by teachers who are to do the implementing, the teachers themselves have created the curriculum probably with instructional aspirations in mind.

Proposition #20

> *Planning, implementation, and evaluation constitute an annual curriculum cycle, and feedback from evaluation efforts plus innovative ideas will produce change in the curriculum with each new cycle.*

This proposition is quite self-explanatory. It is assumed that the planning function never ceases. Experience with implementation and evaluation provides feedback to the planning function for curriculum change. The planning function should provide avenues for the input of ideas from external sources as well as the feedback from internal sources. To some extent, it should be expected that curriculum will be changed each year, that is, each time it is implemented.

Proposition #21

> *The assignment of leadership responsibility and accountability for curriculum engineering functions is mandatory for the perseverance of a curriculum system.*

The functions of a curriculum system are completely dependent upon constant leadership; therefore, responsibility and accountability for them are critical elements of curriculum engineering. Some of our research has shown that the effects of leadership may actually negate other effects of curriculum engineering when the demand for leadership responsibility and accountability is not sustained.

Proposition #22

> *The optimal arena for curriculum planning, implementation, and evaluation is the individual school unit.*

In substance, this proposition is a generalization derived from most of the foregoing propositions on curriculum engineering. Leadership and teaching personnel in a school unit meet each other in a face-to-face situation every day. All may be involved in these curriculum functions readily, and the involvement is facilitated by their singular purpose in the conduct of the school. The significance of problems of articulation among school units within a school district are dimmed by the obvious advantages to be gained by using the individual school as the arena for curriculum functions.

Proposition #23

> *The most obvious and necessary output of a curriculum system is a planned curriculum, and it is the only visible output.*

It is useless to talk about curriculum planning without thinking about what the result of the planning shall be. It is axiomatic to my theory that a curriculum, as an output of a curriculum system, is a written document. The curriculum is the only concretely visible output in that it is substantive and readable. Other outputs, such as improved teacher insight and improved rapport within the teacher group, are more intangible and have to be observed indirectly.

FINAL COMMENT

The above definitions and propositions represent the development of my curriculum theory up to the present time. The definitions are operational for the most part. They have to be if they are to be useful as a directive force for research design. The propositions are axioms, descriptions, assumptions, or generalizations. Some have been tested in research; all are subject to more research. Obviously, research is needed to extend our knowledge of relationships among observed phenomena within the domain of curriculum and to extend our knowledge of relationships among curriculum phenomena and phenomena in other systems of schooling. So far there is a paucity of predictive and causal relationships established, but we are working on them.

Beginning with the first edition of this book in 1961, I have been suggesting that others who purport to be curriculum theorists do the same type of thing I have attempted in this chapter and in this book, namely, to set forth the ingredients of their theories in the form of definitions and other theoretical statements that would lead to research hypotheses to be tested, and subsequently, to generalizations about the curriculum field. One of the main reasons for the chaotic condition of curriculum research is the lack of theory direction in its conduct. There is no reason to search for a single theoretical explanation of curriculum. What is needed are curriculum theories which emanate from different definitions, structures, and propositions so that curriculum events in practice may be guided by rational explanation rather than trial-and-error or bandwagon approaches.

INDEX